I know the face, but . . .

By the same author

**TO SEA IN A SIEVE
BULLS IN THE MEADOWS**

I know the face, but . . .

by
Peter Bull

The Noverre Press

First published in 1959

This edition published in 2022 by
The Noverre Press
Southwold House
Isington Road
Binsted
Hampshire
GU34 4PH

ISBN 978-1-914311-38-3

© 2022 The Noverre Press

To the cast of this book,
not necessarily in order of appearance,
with affection and gratitude.

CONTENTS

I	*"You Ought To Go Off The Stage!"*	9
II	Two Ambitions Quenched in Two Years	28
III	A Slight Case of Mismanagement	47
IV	Muddling through Again	60
V	I Have My Chance (and Miss It)	76
VI	*The Lady's Not for Burning*	96
VII	Success Strikes Again	114
VIII	A Few Fabulous Flops	128
IX	B to Z Films	147
X	*Waiting for Godot*	166
XI	"I know the face, but . . ."	192
XII	The Summing-up	208
	Index	221

Chapter 1

"YOU OUGHT TO GO OFF THE STAGE!"

I HAD better confess at the outset that I am (or perhaps was) an actor. I am telling you this now so that those allergic to theatrical biographies may be spared a return trip to their lending libraries. Not that this is the usual story of "Seven Steps to Stardom" or "Discovered Genius in the West Cromwell Road". It is simply the tale of a busker who is at the crossroads.

For a quarter of a century I have been connected with the theatre, and until very recently was certain that I had no intention of severing the ties which bound me to it. A few years ago, however, I had the good fortune to stumble on a sideline, and thanks to indulgent publishers and you, dear readers, I have been encouraged to pursue this new profession with enthusiasm and indeed financial reward. It is a quieter and less nerve-racking way of making a living, and it is impossible to ignore a whisper that echoes through my brain to the tune of "You ought to go off the stage. You ought to go off the stage."

In my frequent fantasies concerning my obituary I see a simple tombstone or urn with the following inscription on it:

> "HERE LIES PETER BULL
> WHO MISSED THE BUS
> WITHOUT MAKING ANY SERIOUS ATTEMPT
> TO CATCH IT."

And it would be a true epitaph, causing me to reflect that perhaps I have wasted my entire life. Yet I cannot consider myself a tragic figure, having loved the theatrical profession for so long; and this book is to explain to you (and incidentally myself) why I feel any drastic decision must be the outcome of

"I Know the Face, but . . ."

a complete stocktaking. My other aims are: (*a*) to try to discourage those with a tiny talent, or no talent at all, from joining an overcrowded profession, and (*b*) to make enough money to get a step nearer to leaving the stage.

I doubt if I shall succeed in either of these, but while we are waiting to see the outcome, I had better get on with the saga which has put me in such a quandary. But how to begin? I must study other theatrical biographies and see how they cope with this problem.

Yes, I see. I have to trace any hereditary talent. That's easy. No one ever used the magic phrase "You ought to go on the stage" to me, but my Aunt Norah (on my mother's side) was on tour with *The Private Secretary* at the turn of the century, and later understudied in something called *Leah Kleschna* at Drury Lane Theatre, before retiring from the stage at the age of thirty. Her stage name was Nora Gray, a pseudonym which she also adopted for her literary career, during which she wrote very romantic short stories for a publication entitled *The Blue Magazine*, which was not the sort of journal you might think. It is, however, fair to assume that she passed on both her gifts to me.

Other theatrical connections were my Uncle Jocelyn (a tiny uncle, also on my mother's side) who had written several successful plays, had an enormous moustache and liked to feed the pigeons in Trafalgar Square, and a Mme Sarah Bernhardt, whose business affairs were administered by my solicitor grandfather (on my mother's side).

I have not as yet mentioned my father's side, but everyone was on it when he refused point-blank to let me tread what are laughingly known as "The Boards". My desire to plunge into the theatrical world attacked me very early on in life, and even at school I was kept busy writing to actresses for their photographs. These I stuck up in my study until my housemaster ordered me to tear them down. It was 1927 and pride of place went to June, José Collins and, of course, Miss Tallulah

"You Ought to Go Off the Stage!"

Bankhead. My mentor said he would not have the place defiled by actresses, so I stuck up a picture of Mr Paul Robeson which cost me six strokes on the b.t.m. But all this sort of thing made me feel very sophisticated and hardly able to bear my housemaster's lecture on sex to those leaving, which practically began:

"You may have noticed between your legs . . ."

In the holidays I was seldom out of the theatre, and read everything I could lay my hands on about the subject. Yet I knew I did not necessarily want to be an actor. I just desired vaguely to be connected with "the stage". To be someone's secretary or dresser was the sort of appointment I had in view, but my parents did not seem all that keen on the idea. I was packed off post-haste to the University of Tours, where I had an ecstatic five months. The trouble was that I never met any French people and my letters home seem to have created a bad impression. After a vivid account of a fancy-dress dance in which I unwisely described the costumes in which my partner and I were arrayed, my father arrived out of the blue and whisked me back to London where I would have more limited opportunities of appearing as a tomato, accompanied by a young lady in a top hat and virtually nothing else.

My father wanted me to be a chartered accountant, a profession which seemed to me to lack glamour. However, in order to show willing, I did settle for "journalism". Through influence I joined an organisation known in those days as "The Great Eight", consisting as it did of that number of illustrated journals, headed by the *Tatler* and the *Illustrated London News*. In theory I was to work my way through all the departments, and I started by canvassing for advertisements for the *Tatler*, graduating to the editorial columns of this paper, and for an all too brief moment my brother and I were "Eve" of "The Letters of Eve" while someone was on holiday. My bro. was a sort of Débutante's Delight and as such was invited EVERY-

"I Know the Face, but . . ."

WHERE, and thus could give me all the more lurid details of Society which supplemented my contribution. I went to first nights in the gallery with my mother's binoculars, and gave totally incorrect descriptions of What They Were Wearing. Between us, we used to pep up the columns quite a tidge, until a couple of threatened libel actions stopped us being "Eve", and I went back to counting the number of words in the articles.

Later I was transferred to the *Graphic*, which was unfortunately very much on the skids at the time, and shortly after my arrival turned into something called the *National Graphic*, printed on rather common paper, and sold at sixpence a week instead of a shilling. My salary—four pounds a week—happily remained the same, but not for long. The paper passed into oblivion and I left the building. Before I did this, however, I never noticed in the lift a tall, slender, young man going up to the top floor to do a bit of drawing. He turned out afterwards to be Michael Wilding, but as he didn't notice me, the whole of this paragraph is a waste of time, except that I was told by the publishers I must bring in a few star names fairly early on. All theatrical biographies do.

I then went to Odhams Press, where I joined a paper called the *Ideal Home*, for which I was an advertising representative. I hated this job, because it meant my trying to persuade firms into taking space by convincing them that it was worth a vast expenditure. To complicate matters, I had to bring in a certain amount of money every month, which resulted in my going round to my friends about the twenty-ninth of each month and browbeating them into action. My principal friend was an enchanting lady called, then, Susan Tilney, who owned a firm called "Susan's Inventions" which constructed a large number of the most bizarre labour-saving devices that I have clapped my peepers on. One was "The Eiderdowner", which consisted of two clips to keep the eiderdown from slipping off the bed. Then there was the "Dirty Dog Bag" for keeping your dog in if

"You Ought to Go Off the Stage!"

it was wet and muddy, and your own dogs in if they were ditto, if you follow me. A cushion that you strapped on to yourself for use in trains was another ingenious idea, and a "Garden Horse" for sitting on when reading had many devotees, including the late Queen Mary. It was also equipped with numerous sockets and pockets for keeping tools, seeds and hoses in. I remember also a rather snobby stick for attaching money to when one was out hunting and some kind agricultural minion opened the gate to you. Susan Tilney used to travel a great deal by train surrounded by and/or wearing all her inventions, which caused a good measure of curiosity and resultant business. There is no record, however, of her sitting in the corridor astride the "Garden Horse".

But in spite of her generosity and that of other friends in the world of commerce, I was unable to make good, and was sacked from the *Ideal Home*, and this disaster coincided with the death of my father. What to do? I inserted an advertisement in *The Times*, drawing attention to my qualifications, and asking for suggestions. This resulted in one letter from a nudist camp which I didn't follow up. I was by now twenty-one years of age, and, in my opinion, pretty promising material for something. I had an idea that my mother did not mind quite so much about my stage interests as my father had done, and I determined to go ahead. I decided that I must have something called "training", so for a few weeks I had splendid private voice-production lessons from Miss Elsie Fogerty, the doyenne of The Central School of Dramatic Art, which operated in the Royal Albert Hall in those days. The lessons consisted mainly of feeling Miss Fogerty's stomach when she was speaking and her feeling my stomach when I was speaking. It sounds sexy but wasn't. I then bought a copy of her book called "Speechcraft" which I didn't quite understand, and asked her for a bill, which she never gave me. She was a great lady, and it is perhaps fortunate that she did not live long enough actually to catch me at it.

I was by now fully equipped to embark on my stage career, or so I imagined. Not for me the hard way with a talent like mine; no repertory theatres, no fit-up tours, whatever they are, or one-night stands. I was to give myself to London in my full glory, and wrote off to every manager whose address I could find. My best bet was Charles B. Cochran, who had been a client of Bull and Bull and a close friend of my father, and he very kindly got his production manager, the late Frank Collins, to give me the once-over. Mr Collins quite rightly suggested that I should get a bit of experience before playing a leading part in a Cochran production, so I graciously said I would.

To my amazement Sydney Carroll, to whom I had also written, sent for me and, after introducing me to his director, Maxwell Wray, gave me thirty shillings a week and at least two non-speaking parts in a play called *If I Were You*. The piece, which was about Jewish pogroms in Russia, opened on June 15th, 1933, and ran for every one of eight performances at the now defunct Shaftesbury Theatre. Owing to the number of tickets I dished out for the first night, I was a good deal out of pocket by the end of the run. I played a noisy Russian student in the first act swinging an empty champagne bottle round my head, and a very old janitor in the last act. As I have always gone the whole hog with character make-up, without any knowledge to back the hog up, my make-up bills were stupendous. I was, of course, completely recognisable in both roles.

Also in the cast were Augustus Yorke, the original Potash or Perlmutter in the play of those names, and a wonderful old character actress called Joan Pereira, who was to have a big effect on my career. Playing a student in the first act and a policeman in the third was the now famous director, Frith Banbury. He spent a lot of money on make-up too, but had been

"You Ought to Go Off the Stage!"

fully trained, or so he said, and impressed me enormously. We became great friends, and every night each of us took one arm of Joan Pereira across the road in order to catch her bus. There were only six buses in actual fact, because she did not go home after the two matinées. The first night was attended by a large proportion of my family and friends, none of whom were committal about the play or my chances of achieving stardom overnight. The last night was attended, as far as I can remember, by no one at all.

Frith and I were out of work as a result, but we had no intention of "resting", and we decided to get into some Sunday shows while awaiting our next assortment of roles. In those days there were a great many societies banging away on Sunday nights, and they were not taken as seriously as they are now. A few reputable ones like the Repertory Players were in existence, but they were highly professional and not a suitable playground for beginners. We did manage, however, to get into a lovely play called *Dath* which was put on by The 1930 Players in 1933 for two pretty astonishing performances at the Ambassadors Theatre. It was about ancient Britain, and was written by Miss Bertha Graham, the chairlady of The 1930 Players. Frith played a captain of the army and I was most of the army for most of the rehearsals. Indeed, I can well remember him saying: "Are you with me, men?" to which I replied, "Yes." I think it was my best line.

Also in the cast were Catherine Lacey, Leo Genn, Harold Clayton, and a loaf of bread which, for reasons best known to itself, rolled about the stage a great deal during the Monday matinée and caused vast merriment both sides of the footlights. By Monday the news had spread round the theatrical profession like a forest fire and the theatre was crammed from top to bottom with earnest students of contemporary drama. Miss Graham had brought in a lot of her friends to play captive lady Britons, and I had to bind them up a good deal, which was very

"I Know the Face, but . . ."

difficult as they struggled like maniacs, not having attended many rehearsals. I remember many notable lines in the play, and it is difficult to forget a character called Eine, the Herb-Woman, played with élan by Miss Inez Bensusan, who at the dress-rehearsal had forgotten a fairly essential "prop", and announced on the stage, "I am Eine, the Herb-Woman". There was then a long pause before she hissed into the wings, "I've forgotten the herbs", which were thrown on by the distraught stage-manager, and the set suddenly resembled Culpepper House. Other lines that stick in one's memory are, "Brazen, the Tall, bring up the rear"; and "Agg, let us go fishing in the lower pool". The latter line was assigned to Mr Banbury, who for obvious reasons found it rather difficult to deliver at the second performance. The entrance of the captive lady Britons was heralded by, "Who are these in gorgeous raiment?" which was a slight case of the misapplied adjective. For Miss Graham had ransacked her attic and/or bottom drawers for the company, and everything from deer's antlers to Victorian button boots was being handsomely displayed.

After this extravagant exercise, Frith and I went from strength to strength and got splendidly involved in an organisation known as "The Tempest Theatre" which was run by two young gentlemen, one of Swedish extraction, who took themselves v. seriously indeed. Readings took place on the third floor of a house in Percy Street to the accompaniment of a strong smell of frankincense and myrrh and some rather hairy nuts which were offered between the acts. They organised entertainments for Sunday nights at the Fortune Theatre, and the first one in which I appeared was called *Perdican and Camilla* about which I can remember very little, but the play was preceded by an unforgettable lady called Valeska Gert who mimed everything including, I regret to say, "Being A Baby". This consisted largely of blowing bubbles out of her mouth, which plunged the audience into ecstasy and caused her to run off shouting "Ich habe

"You Ought to Go Off the Stage!"

nimmer getanzt für eine solche Publik" or some such phrase. However, she did say to Mr Banbury, "Ich finde das Bull ist gut als komiker", which Frith still puts in some of his first-night telegrams to me.

The Tempest Theatre's next contribution to the history of the drama was a German play called *Leonce and Lena*, which provided me with the part of either King Pipi of Popo or King Popo of Pipi. It was a very big part and I was given dressing-room No 1 at the Fortune Theatre, but I was not helped in my rendering of the role by Mr Banbury who was playing the subsidiary part of The Chancellor and kept on saying, "Tut, tut, your Majesty", whether it was in the script or not. The producer, Herr Mellinger, had been rather sharp during rehearsals, and had once said to Mr Banbury, "You must not make nonsense with yourself, Mr Banbury", whatever that could possibly mean. The dress-rehearsal was a notable one, as he had engaged a lot of art school students to what's known as "walk-on" in the production. He was not entirely prepared to find that these artistes had walked off and were indulging in what can only be described as sexual intercourse underneath the stage. This gave a slightly ragged touch to the dress-rehearsal, during which Mrs Louis Kentner (a darling and lovely lady then called Griselda Gould) fell through a soap box not once but twice. She had also to do a good deal of running in order to avoid being pinched by at least two of the character actors and those of the art school who were not otherwise employed. The behaviour of Miss Gould, Mr Banbury and myself throughout this production unfortunately prevented us from being asked to appear in any other Tempest Theatre project, and one of the directors married Miss Valeska Gert.

Mr Banbury and I then had to part company, and he went into a series of commercial productions. I, on the other hand, joined the extreme *avant-garde* theatre of this time, viz. the Gate Theatre Studio in Villiers Street, a tiny building of enor-

"I Know the Face, but . . ."

mous reputation and minute salaries. The sanitary arrangements for the artistes were plain and simple, as buckets were cheerfully provided in each of the dressing-rooms (two). I obtained this job entirely through the efforts of Miss Joan Pereira who rang me up and ordered me to report to Mr Peter Godfrey, who was at that time running the theatre. She was pretty cryptic on the blower, and instructed me to say "Yes" when Mr Godfrey asked me if I spoke German. As the only German I knew had been picked up from Valeska Gert or Mr Banbury imitating Valeska Gert, I could not help thinking that I was courting disaster, but off I tootled to be given a script of *As You Desire Me* by Pirandello. I was to study the part of the doctor in the last act and to come back after lunch and read it to Mr Godfrey. Mystified and alarmed by the discovery that the entire role was in German, I stood about wondering what to do for the best when Miss Pereira emerged from the lady's loo (for the use of the audience usually), and told me to meet her in the ABC up the street in ten mins. I carried out her instructions, and Joan taught me the part parrot-fashion over "poached eggs on toast twice". I went back, read it to the bearded Mr Godfrey, accepted the one pound a week offered as salary, and decided that I was an actor at last.

The cast was a highly distinguished one in the light of what has since occurred. It was headed by one of the most exciting personalities I have ever known, Jean Forbes-Robertson, who moved me so much in the play that I used to find myself trying to stop the tears coming to my eyes on the stage, which would not quite have fitted in with the character of the phlegmatic German doctor I was meant to portray. Also in the cast were Alastair Sim, Glen Byam-Shaw and Alan Webb. The maximum salary at the theatre was three pounds a week. I kept mousy quiet about my lack of German until one night I was summoned by Miss Forbes-R., who was not a one to mince matters.

"You don't understand a word of German, do you, Peter?"

"You Ought to Go Off the Stage!"

she asked bluntly. I saw my pound a week vanishing in front of my eyes, but she had called me Peter.

"No," I admitted. Miss Forbes-R. roared with laughter, and that was all that happened until the next evening's performance. I came on to the stage to deliver my opening line which was "Hat sie eine rote Nabe auf ihre Brüste?", which means (or so Joan Pereira assured me), "Has she a red mark on her bust?" I delivered the line as best I could under the circumstances. The circumstances included Miss F-R. and Messrs Webb and Byam-Shaw trembling on the brink of hysterical laughter. I got through the rest of my lines in a high falsetto and made a not very graceful exit. It was my first contact with the appalling malady which affects most actors, and which is almost impossible to explain to laymen. Something which does not seem remotely funny to the onlooker or even in retrospect, can plunge whole casts into hysteria, and a scene, or indeed a whole play, may be wrecked by a tiny untoward slip of the tongue or the behaviour of a hitherto inanimate object.

As a result, I came to dread doing the scene and was bitterly ashamed of myself. One night, after a deplorable exhibition, the Messrs Webb, B-S., and I stayed behind, just saying the lines over and over again, laughing like maniacs until we were tired and bored. Needless to say, next night I was off like a soda-water siphon once more.

As You Desire Me was a great success, and we ran six weeks to packed houses, and during the run I was summoned by the great Charles Cochran himself, who said that his Mr Collins had seen me in the piece (it must have been one of my comparatively normal nights) and had reported favourably. He was prepared, he said, to offer me a minute part or parts and/or an understudy in one of his two forthcoming productions. The choice was between an adaptation of Louis Golding's *Magnolia Street* which was to be done in a very spectacular way by Komisarjevsky, or a play starring Elisabeth Bergner, who was

"I Know the Face, but..."

about to make her début in England in Margaret Kennedy's *Escape Me Never*, adapted from her book *The Fool of The Family*. Komisarjevsky was also to direct this, and as I had just seen Bergner in a film called *Der Traumende Mund*, and thought her nothing short of miraculous, the choice was an easy one. In actual fact *Magnolia Street* ran only six weeks, and *Escape Me Never* was to keep me fully employed for about two years.

I was to be paid four pounds ten shillings per week and the only part specified in my contract was that of a waiter. Flushed with excitement, before rehearsals I started taking lessons both in French and German from my friend Joan Pereira, who was about vingty-lingual, in her flat in the Vauxhall Bridge Road. I was not allowed to speak anything but German or French from the moment she opened the door, and our conversation was in consequence pretty peculiar. Miss Pereira would say "Ich habe die Molly Hamley-Clifford in das Arts Theatre Club gesehen", which meant that she had met another character actress called Molly Hamley-Clifford in the Arts Theatre Club. (Or perhaps you'd guessed that?) But all this training was to come in extremely useful when I played parts like the German Captain in *The African Queen* in full German (subsequently dubbed by Walter Rilla).

Rehearsals for *Escape Me Never* started in October 1933 and were vastly exciting. The first one was held at His Majesty's Theatre and the cast seemed enormous. There were some distinguished names to bandy around, like Leon Quartermaine, Hugh Sinclair, dear old Katie Johnson, and the splendid Edgar Wallace actor called Cronin Wilson.

Miss Bergner had us all at her feet from the moment she passed through the swing doors, tiny in an enormous fur coat. It wasn't until later that she also brought her huge sheepdog who was called Boompsie. She was to revolutionise my ideas about acting, as most of her effects were made either with her

"You Ought to Go Off the Stage!"

back to the audience or standing stock still with the minimum of gesture. We were to open at the Opera House, Manchester, and before we arrived there, the whole undertaking was underplayed and there was very little advance publicity. But the first-night audience in Manchester cheered the place down, and Miss Bergner took about twenty solo calls. The next day the papers were ringing her praises, and it was quite obvious that we were in for a great success. She was in those early days quite petrified with nerves and misery, and I, in the role of a very old porter, with beard and fairly full character make-up, had to carry her on for her first entrance. I sometimes had to pursue her from the far corner of the stage, or even her dressing-room.

The first night in London was one of those legendary affairs that really happened. We opened at the Apollo Theatre on December 8th, 1933, and it was very difficult to get the audience to leave the theatre. I remember Elisabeth B. in the coffee-stall scene saying under her breath, "They don't like it, they don't like it", but within a few minutes it was patent that she had made one of the biggest successes in theatrical history. It was to be an hilarious, happy and sensational run. I was kept busy changing from being an old porter into a young waiter, and then a singing customer at a coffee-stall. As usual, all three roles were clearly recognisable from the front. I had a line or two as the waiter, and one got "a Laugh". My whole existence in those days hinged on the public's reaction to the laugh line, which I tabulated in my diary every night, giving myself marks out of a hundred. The scene took place on an hotel terrace in the Dolomites and two middle-aged English spinsters were fumbling in their phrase-books. Finally, "Due caffè neri", they said to the plumpish waiter. The plumpish waiter replied, "Two black coffees, yes, madam" in faultless English. Money for old rope.

This was the part of the play I liked best. After Miss Bergner had settled down and relaxed a bit, she gave the old porter in

"I Know the Face, but..."

the first act some pretty rough handling, particularly at matinées. She used to tear his beard and moustache off, and throw them on the floor, leaving him facing upstage naked and giggling. I got my own back in the second act by bringing her and Hugh Sinclair a bill, on which I used to write tiny obscenities in the hope of making them laugh. They remained frozen-faced at my efforts until I went a hundred and forty-five times too far by writing on the bill one matinée: "Two lumps of bull —price 2s. 6d." Miss Bergner, in a crystal-clear voice which rang through the old-ladies-filled audience, said: "What does bull mean, Sebastian?", knowing perfectly well the answer. Bedlam ensued, and I got the sack from the rightly livid stage-director. Miss Bergner intervened and I was reinstated, and for at least two perfs. wrote quite ordinary things on the bill, which made me even more hysterical.

The run was nothing if not eventful, and at the end of three months an astonishing thing happened. Elisabeth was taken suddenly ill during the first act and when she should have made her entrance, the curtain was lowered. Her understudy was a charming and talented girl called Betty Lynne, who had won the Gold Medal at the Royal Academy of Dramatic Art. She had made a small success as the pathetic chambermaid in *Grand Hotel*, and from what I had seen at understudy rehearsals was more than capable of giving an exciting performance. But on this occasion, "The Theatre" was at its cruellest. The management decided to suspend the run until Miss Bergner's recovery, the curtain was rung down, Hugh Sinclair had to make a speech explaining the illness of our star, money was returned to the audience, and Miss Lynne's theatrical heart was broken. Shortly afterwards she left the stage.

But for the rest of the cast, the suspension was a fortunate one. We were all put on half-pay, and I went off on a holiday to Cornwall, and ended up at a small seaside resort called Perranporth. This event was to reshape my whole life, because two

"You Ought to Go Off the Stage!"

years later, with Robert Morley, Roger and Judith Furse, Frith Banbury and others, I was to run a summer theatre in the Women's Institute, which was to provide us all with son fairly remarkable experiences. It is another story, and frank another book (memo. for my dear publishers), but as a "trailer" I would like to provide one or two extraordinary facts about the enterprise.

The stage at the beginning of our tenancy measured just six and a half feet by twelve, which slightly restricted movement. This handicap was increased by the fact that there was only one proper exit, apart from the back door of the actual building, which came in the middle of the stage and led straight into the backyard. This meant that on wet nights we had to provi˙ a "duty watch" of umbrella-carriers for those using this mo of exit.

Except for a carpenter there were no salaried personnel, and there was a general dish-out of profits at the end of the season. As the hall held only two hundred seats, the margin was narrow. But I took a house for the season, and provided board, lodging, hairdressing, haircuts, Cornish cream and indeed the highest teas ever served in the Western Hemisphere. The whole thing worked out pretty miraculously owing to the talents and dispositions of those with whom I was associated. It was, I think, the only repertory theatre in England to have occasional hampers from Fortnum and Mason's, and certainly the only one where the larger members of the cast (no names, no pack drill) had to go round testing the deck-chairs before each performance. This involved having to PRETEND to be rolling out of one's seat with laughter in order to give it a proper rehearsal.

The work involved was tremendous, because at one time we were doing four plays a week, but later in the season we kept on repeating the programme to fit in with the influx of fresh visitors. We did three brand-new plays, one of which, *Goodness, How Sad!* was written for the company by Robert Morley

"*I Know the Face, but . . .*"

and played in London subsequently, for eight months. But that also is another story, and I must go back to the Apollo Theatre to resume my three roles in *Escape Me Never*.

We had had a four weeks' lay-off, and the next startling event of the run was the tragedy of Cronin Wilson. He was plainly very ill indeed, but insisted on continuing until one night he found himself on the stage fighting for breath and unable to utter. It was a scene with Hugh Sinclair, who gave on this occasion the most remarkable virtuoso performance that I can remember. He managed to twist his own lines so that the plot was sustained, and the audience actually noticed nothing wrong. But poor Cronin Wilson had played his last scene, and died in his dressing-room later that night. Tristram Rawson took over, and continued to play until the autumn. There was never even an empty box, and we were naturally flabbergasted when the notice suddenly went up. Apparently Miss Bergner was tired and was committed to a film in the near future. She had, however, promised Cochran that she would appear in New York in the play the following year, and that was that.

We were all deeply upset and, I regret to say, felt hard done-by. But in conclave with some other members of the company, a pretty peculiar plan for our reimbursement was devised. We bought up every ticket we could lay our hands on for the last night from the box-office and the agents, advertised our wares in *The Times*, and took a furnished flat in Old Burlington Gardens to carry out our nefarious business. We engaged a sinister messenger to open and close the door, take the actual cash and run out in the streets to bring us double brandies. At first the demand was splendid, and we even got as much as ten pounds for a thirteen-and-sixpence stall, but suddenly the bottom dropped out of the market and we found ourselves faced with a lot of empty seats on our hands. The last day of all, to cut our losses, we sold some of them at cost price, and raced to the theatre in

"You Ought to Go Off the Stage!"

order to play our roles for what amounted to a highly personal audience.

Mr Cochran had inserted a slip in the programme dissociating himself from our iniquity, and I wonder what he would have said to the goings on outside Drury Lane Theatre this day and age. (I am referring to a musical play, the title of which is *My Fair Lady*.)[1] It was actually a sad evening for all of us, and I seem to recall bursting into tears at one period of the evening, feeling that I would never have a happier and more glamorous engagement again. I didn't know that it was nowhere near the end of *Escape Me Never* as far as I was concerned.

For the next few months, I set about getting all the work I could find. I made my film début in something called *The Secret Voice*, which was so secret that it only made the Broadway Gardens Cinema in Walham Green one Sunday night. I got involved in a fairly off-beat theatre in South Kensington, which was started by a lot of Chelsea residents, including the entire Furse family, Anthony Quayle, Andrew Cruickshank, Reginald Beckwith, Nicholas Phipps, among others. Perfs. took place in the Imperial Institute Cinema, and one had to pass a lot of curious exhibits on the way to one's seat. They did *Anna Christie* and *Liebelei*, and I wedged myself into a faintly improper play called *I Was Waiting For You* which didn't actually set South Ken. on fire. But there were some very funny and delightful people connected with the venture, which made it a happy engagement.

The next improbable set-up with which I got connected was the Left Theatre, who produced plays which were Communist propaganda of the most violent sort. I enjoyed them hugely. We played the Phoenix Theatre for two Sundays in succession, and then did the rounds of the Town Halls, ranging from Stepney to Battersea. I carried a copy of the *Tatler* with me every-

[1] Advt.

"I Know the Face, but . . ."

where to avoid misunderstanding, and played Capitalist Pigs who always got their comeuppance before the end of the evening. The financial reward was slightly above the normal Sunday play "expenses", and it was comforting to have people come up after the performance saying, they had got the Message. The plays were produced by a splendid lady dictator called Barbara Nixon, and were meaty stuff crammed with court scenes, prison scenes and a great many parts. The two productions with which I was associated were *Peace on Earth* and *Mother*.

At the risk of involving all those concerned, including myself, with the UnBritish Activities Tribunal, I would like to draw your attention to the programme of Gorki's *Mother*. I find that I played "Court Official", "Village Police Officer" and "Prosecuting Attorney". I remember the last role best, because it was when beating the hell out of it at either the Islington or East Ham Town Hall that I fell through several soap boxes with a clatter that collapsed the cast, and some of the floor of the Islington or East Ham Town Hall, and, I believe, converted a great number of political waverers. The action of Act One took place in "The Mother's Cottage", "A Cemetery" and "Outside The Factory Gates", which will probably give you some idea of the plot. I do remember certain members of the cast, like Mark Dignam, André Van Gyseghem and Tony Beckwith, but I can't actually put faces to Dorrit Pemberton, Winnie Osgood, A. Goldstein, R. Katz, J. Yason, or indeed, I'm sorry to say, S. Yason. But of course Ben Vynreb was the assistant stage-manager, and it says in the acknowledgements, "Red Flag kindly lent by the Group Theatre", which was very civil of them.

After these capers, *Escape Me Never* popped up again, to my huge delight. First, I was asked to play one of my original parts (The Gent At The Coffee Stall) in the film, but alas and alack, like so many of my contributions to the Bioscope, I was left

"You Ought to Go Off the Stage!"

making faces on the cutting-room floor. But later in the year (1935), I was summoned to the Cochran office and asked to go to New York in the play. I was amazed and once more at Miss Bergner's tiny feet, as apparently she had refused to go unless the entire company went with her. I was to get fifty dollars a week, which in those days was quite adequate as a living wage. We played a limited season at the Shubert Theatre, and Elisabeth repeated her triumph. I was engaged as her personal bodyguard, in order to escort her through the wild fans who congregated outside the Stage Door.

I was fascinated by New York, terrified by the pace and noise, and lived first at a not very old-fashioned hotel, where they lodged you for a fixed price and threw breakfast in. And when I say "threw breakfast in", I mean threw breakfast in. It was done through a slot in the door, and was enclosed in a large cardboard box. A friend of mine found a mouse in his, and when he politely said he would prefer not to have a mouse with his breakfast, they asked him to leave. Later, I moved to a strange apartment where I slept in a cupboard, and was relieved and delighted when the run came to an end, and I could return to quiet, dreary London.

I only came back with four ambitions in mind: to learn a little about acting (if poss.), to go to Hollywood, to have my own theatre, and not to be a star. All these I achieved in three years, with varying results.

Chapter II

TWO AMBITIONS QUENCHED IN TWO YEARS

AFTER my visit to New York, my immediate aim was to secure employment in a Repertory Theatre, where I hoped to bamboozle them a bit with my American reputation. But it was not easy, and there were the usual stumbling-blocks of entire companies already engaged for entire seasons, etc. After a series of abortive attempts I managed to wangle a Special Week at the Opera House, Coventry, in *Clive of India*. The casting for "extra parts" was done from a strange little office in St Martin's Lane run by a witty lady, now unhappily deceased, called Mrs Nelson King, the mother of Meriel Forbes (Lady Richardson). I was to receive Four Guineas (less commission) for the week and something for rehearsals, and arrived full of ambition and determination to Make Good.

The theatre was then run by a genial and brilliant director called Gardner Davies, who was married to a charming young lady entitled, unbelievably, Miss Tina Dewsnap. His assistant was Geoffrey Staines, who subsequently ran York Repertory Theatre, one of the foremost in this country. Mr Staines married Pauline Letts, who played for me during two Perranporth seasons after starting her career at Coventry with an abundance of talent. Other members of the company during my stay there were Judy Campbell, John Robinson, James Hayter, someone called Eileen Tingle and a dear little man called Hwfa Pryse (later Hugh Pryse) of such astonishing versatility that he was able to play the title roles in *A Hundred Years Old* and *Young Woodley* on two successive weeks. His death a few years ago robbed the stage of an enchanting personality.

Two Ambitions Quenched in Two Years

I sucked up like mad to the powers that were during *Clive of India*, and was allowed not only to stay on for the next play (*White Cargo*, as it turned out) but indeed for six months. Looking back on this era arouses in me what is popularly supposed to happen when one reflects on one's years at school. As the latter were and are among my unhappiest memories, it is delightful to think of my time at Coventry as "The Happiest Days of My Career". Indeed, I honestly believe they were, because I was at that susceptible age when the *camaraderie* and efficiency of a happily united company doing really good work caused great enthusiasm and an inward glow. The standard at this particular theatre was remarkable considering we played twice nightly and changed the play weekly. How the leading players are able to face a new script every Tuesday morning is one of the unsolved mysteries of Repertory. I fear this problem never applied to me, as I was never entrusted with a major role and was indeed given so many "Butlers" that I eventually bought a morning-suit at Burtons to avoid embarrassment to myself and more especially the costumiers, who were always being asked at the last moment to find clothes to fit my improbable measurements.

In *White Cargo* it was I who had to give the immortal answer to the question "What, no Cargo?", to which I replied, "Yes. White Cargo" (fairly quick curtain). This line had to be delivered in a steady rock-like voice and I was not assisted by what the Ship's Engineer (Mr James Hayter) was a doing of at the time. I was playing the Captain and used to try to avoid looking anywhere near the Ship's E. who, I regret to say, had turned upstage to me by now, displaying to the actors his opened shirt, which disclosed a painted face on his chest with a cigarette, as if by magic, merrily smoking away in his navel. I still think twice before accepting any engagement in any medium if Mr Hayter is anywhere near the cast list, as he is one

"I Know the Face, but . . ."

of the few people who can send me into paroxysms of mirth just by crossing his eyes, as is his wont.

After I had worked myself into becoming a semi-permanent member of the company I relaxed a bit. I was to be paid £4 for the weeks I worked and £2 for the ones when I didn't. I also found myself doing a good deal of cooking for the Messrs Staines and Davies which helped to solidify my position. I lived at a very droll pub called the Smithfield, opposite the theatre, where a lot of the headliners from the variety theatre, the Hippodrome, used to lodge. I was to meet naturally many colourful personalities there, including Nora Williams the Whistling Songstress, an enchanting electric guitarist called Ken Harvey who was mad on electric trains as well, and Larry Adler, who once played "The Flight of the Bumble Bee" on his harmonica to me in a car outside Kenilworth Castle.

We presented several brand-new plays at Coventry, although none of them got much further. I was in one called *England Expects* which not surprisingly was about Nelson and written by a gentleman called Edgar Middleton, who had previously contributed a jolly sexy play called *Potiphar's Wife*. The Nelson one was very long indeed and not sexy at all. On the Monday night the second house, led by the Mayor of Coventry, staggered wearily away around midnight. Towards the end of a seemingly endless run I suppose I wasn't concentrating as much as I should have been. Anyhow, the line I should have uttered as a sailor aboard the *Victory* was "The *Leviathan* has been sunk". I said on this particular occasion, "The *Lusitania* has been sunk" which seemed to confuse everyone. After the performance a large gentleman came round with my sponsor, Mrs Nelson King, to see us all. Mrs N.-K. wisely kept her trap shut about her protégé, but the large gent said to me with a sweet smile:

"Yours was, I think, the worst performance I've ever seen on any stage." It was of course Robert Morley.

Two Ambitions Quenched in Two Years

He was actually dead right, but I do remember giving a series of excruciating performances while at Coventry. Perhaps the tops in this category was my Old Butler in *March Hares*, though I was treated abominably by the rest of the cast in this production. There was for instance the night when I went to pick up James Hayter's suitcases (usually empty). On this occasion they were practically immobile, as Mr H. had filled them to the brim with stage weights. Later in the week I went deaf in one ear, after bathing in an over-chlorinated swimming-pool, but this unfortunate mishap should not have impelled the company to bellow at me as if I was stone-deaf, which indeed I was after two performances of this sort of thing.

A few weeks later *The Midshipmaid* came sailing over the horizon, in which play I had, for reasons best known to the authors, to play the back legs of a horse during the action. (A pretend-horse of course.) Now this specialised role is not a comfortable one at the best of times, and as I suffer from claustrophobia I tried to secure the part of the front legs. But it was not to be, and to make matters worse it was midsummer and Front Legs, I regret to report, broke wind during one of the perfs. To light a cigarette INSIDE a horse's skin is a v. difficult operation and I am afraid I lost my temper, hit the bottom of Front Legs, forced him to break into a gallop and we had a blazing row (slightly muffled) which didn't help the audience to follow the plot.

The next week wasn't much better and just as claustrophobic, though less smelly. Actually I had a week-out in theory, but they asked me if I'd mind playing the clock in *Ten Minute Alibi*. If you have seen the play and remember it at all, you will know that the entire plot depends on the rendering and behaviour of The Clock. Some poor person has to stand inside the clock, making the necessary adjustments. I completely lost my head on the first night and moved the hands round twenty minutes instead of the required ten, which immediately rendered the

"I Know the Face, but ..."

play gibberish and split up a good many Coventry marriages as couples argued their way back after the performance. It could not go on like this and my understudy was put on for the remainder of the week.

I realised my days at Coventry were numbered, and after a not very convincing display as a Glee-Singer in *The Farmer's Wife*, was told regretfully that my engagement was to be terminated. I left the theatre with a lot of presents, some valuable friendships, and a firm conviction that I was not really fitted for repertory work. Many of the company soon established themselves in various fields, and Gardner Davies was to direct many big successes in the West End until his early death (in a tragic fall from the balcony of the Richmond Theatre) cut short a brilliant career.

Back in London I found a lot of assorted work. There were small parts in films and I broke into TV, in those days an exciting and unpredictable medium, far cosier than it is now. But the most important thing that happened was the cementing of an enduring friendship with Robert Morley, who was to exert such an influence on my life. He was and is the wittiest man I know and, although a great many people seem to find him rather frightening, to me his great kindness, generosity and loyalty more than compensate for his unorthodox approach to the Muse.

He was at this time a comparatively unknown actor who had written a first play entitled *Short Story*, which had been accepted by the firm of H. M. Tennent. The cast they procured for this piece included Marie Tempest, Sybil Thorndike, Ursula Jeans, Margaret Rutherford and two young actors called A. E. Matthews and Rex Harrison. So Mr Morley was sitting fairly pretty, particularly as the director was named Tyrone Guthrie.

But he still rather enjoyed acting in those days and was willing to do anything that cropped up, and there is an endearing

Two Ambitions Quenched in Two Years

story of him walking down Lisle Street (off Leicester Square) in a haze of pleasure, having just fixed a job, when he was accosted by a pretty but rather over-painted member of the feminine sex.

"Doing anything, dear?" she asked.

"Oh yes," replied Mr Morley, swelling out with pride, "I'm just going out on tour as a Pirate in *Treasure Island*."

When I planned my first Perranporth Summer Theatre Season he agreed to come down and act roles as assigned. He was wonderfully co-operative and was persuaded to play the really terrible part of the comic, Tim Bobbin, in *Maria Marten, or Murder in the Red Barn*. This was to be my last production of this season and was not really a happy experiment, though Richard Ainley was pretty spectacular as the dastardly William Corder. Robert was desperately unhappy in his role and I had to give him five shillings a night in order to purchase sweets to bribe the audience into oblivion while he was on. But the ordeal was so soul-shattering to Mr Morley that on the last night of all he gave his entire make-up box, consisting of a stick of five greasepaint, a stick of nine, one powder puff and some pretty sinister crêpe hair to Richard Ainley and announced his immediate resignation from the acting profession. It was no job for a gentleman, he said, and his mother had been right. Henceforth he would write exclusively and not have to prostitute himself.

A few weeks previously he had advised Frith Banbury not to play a part in the Stokes' play on Oscar Wilde which was about to be put on at the Gate Theatre Studio by Norman Marshall. It could only be presented at a theatre of this type as the Lord Chamberlain had banned it. Mr Morley had advised Mr Banbury not on any account to accept the engagement as it would do him irreparable harm to be associated with such a venture and such a play. Mr Banbury listened with great attention and clinched the deal, but I think even Robert was mildly surprised

"I Know the Face, but . . ."

a few weeks later to find himself playing the title role (viz. Oscar Wilde) in that very production. This step was to start him off on his meteoric career, as he made a sensational success in the play, to be repeated a few months later at the Fulton Theatre, New York.

But even this did not prevent him from coming back to Perranporth the following year for the second season and for peanuts (or rather Cornish Cream, as it turned out). He had also found time to write a play specially for the little theatre, *Goodness, How Sad!*, to which we gave a "World Première" on July 26th, 1937. It was directed there by the author and we were all pretty mad about it. Luckily the audiences seemed to share our enthusiasm and I was determined to get it to London as quickly as possible. But there were a lot of snags, mainly financial, to be overcome, and in the middle of our struggles to achieve our desires Robert was invited to Holywood to make final tests for a film called *Marie Antoinette* in which it was proposed that he should play Louis XVI. It seemed a chance not to be missed, and I saw him off at Waterloo Station rather gloomily. I'm always better at offensive action if someone is there to goad me, and I could see myself drowning the chances of the play in a morass of lethargy and incompetence.

Luckily a few days later I was given an ideal opportunity to procrastinate when the long arm of coincidence stretched out and my phone went with some startling news from the other end of the blower. It was my agents, who rather vaguely inquired if I was interested in making some preliminary tests for a Hollywood film. "Yes," I said. "What film?"

"*Marie Antoinette*," they replied.

"What part?" I asked.

"The King."

I told them that I had only recently seen the King off on a Southern Railway train and they said they would investigate further.

Two Ambitions Quenched in Two Years

Later Mr Harold Huth, then in charge of all M.G.M. tests in England, rang me up to tell me that he had received a cryptic cable from California which read, "Make test of Peter Bull as Gamin". As he had no script handy and indeed confessed that he had never heard the word "Gamin" except as applicable to some of Miss Elisabeth Bergner's performances, he was in a slight quandary. I am bound to say that at this period my chances seemed anything but rosy, but somehow I thought it was worth an effortette and darted off to the British Museum, where I had a friend in the Library, who handed me down a lot of heavy tomes about the French Rev. After many hours' study I elucidated the undoubted fact that Gamin was Louis XVI's rather common blacksmith friend, who poisoned people on the side. It wasn't much of a help really, as he appeared to be rather a shadowy figure. However, I reported my findings to Mr Huth, who said he would test me but perhaps I would like to write the script. Now this was quite a turn-up for the book, as very few people, except Emlyn W., N. Coward and Mr Morley are allowed to say what they write, and I knew for a fact that Mr Morley on this occasion had had to say Other People's Lines, so I basked in my luck and tore off a very showy little scene with no other characters. It was difficult to do and I made myself go a bit potty at the end to help the viewer, and Mr Huth directed me with sympathy and understanding. I did the test at Elstree where the studios for the past few months had been littered with Louis XVI's of various distinctions and one King of France had actually bumped into another in the corridor. But I was relieved to find no sign of another Gamin, did my lot and disappeared back to London. For months I heard nothing, although later it transpired that my test, and that of the late Francis L. Sullivan (as Louis XVI), had come down in an aeroplane in the middle of the Arizona desert. I hung on as long as I could, encouraged by long letters from Robert saying how

"I Know the Face, but . . ."

excruciatingly funny it was out there, but finally had to set about getting work of some sort.

I still couldn't raise the capital for *Goodness, How Sad!*, and was suddenly asked by Norman Marshall to compère his annual Gate Theatre Studio revue. These were very chic affairs, starring Hermione Gingold, whose immense talents were then apparently only recognised by the faithful habitués of the tiny theatre. It sounded an exciting idea and I was keen to do it. Reginald Beckwith and my oldest friend in the world, Nicholas Phipps, were writing most of the material, and it was proposed that I should wander on and off dressed as Father Time and have terrible rows with J. B. Priestley (to be played by Beckwith) about being tampered with. It must be explained that 1937 was the year when Priestley had two big successes on in London, called *Time and the Conways* and *I Have been Here Before*, both of which dealt with the time factor.

A very amusing company had been engaged and I was really rather looking forward to it all, but in some obscure way could not believe that I would ever actually open in the revue. So I was not altogether surprised when my agent, the late Vere Barker, summoned me during rehearsals and drove me in his black Rolls to the M.G.M. office in Lower Regent Street. Here Mr Ben Goetz received us in most friendly fashion and was unwise enough to leave the room for a few seconds during the interview. It was thus easy for my long-sighted eyes to read the cable which lay on the desk and read quite simply: "Get Bull on next boat." I was in consequence very over-excited, but Mr Barker managed to be sufficiently off-hand with Mr Goetz on his return to make my blood curdle but to secure for me a splendid and generous contract.

Mr Marshall and the cast of the revue forgave me and I left almost immediately on the *Normandie*, I mean *in* the *Normandie*, where of course I won the table-tennis competition, beating M. Charles Boyer in the opening round. I finished

Two Ambitions Quenched in Two Years

the voyage in a coma of good living and was not sick once. As Bob Ritchie, Jeanette Macdonald's then current husband and Mr Goetz' right-hand man, had pointed out to me, "Ben Goetz is practically king of the *Normandie*," which indeed was proved by the accommodation provided. On arrival at New York I was met by a posse of gents from Metro-Goldwyn-Mayer, who were slightly taken aback by my old trunk exploding as it descended the chute in the Customs Yard. However they shepherded me about New York during the day, and I had tea with Mr and Mrs Charles B. Cochran, and left for California by air that evening. I was met at the airport by R. Morley and Llewellyn Rees. The latter, who had just finished an engagement with *George and Margaret* in New York, had decided to stay on in America and had unwisely said he would be our chauffeur and companion in Hollywood during the winter months. He put up with a good deal of sauce from us both, and our general behaviour both at the dinner and the card table left a certain amount to be desired.

Mr Morley was wearing a nice blue sports jacket; not, you may think, a very sensational bit of information to convey to you, but I would point out that I was disporting its twin, having bought the only possible coat (figuratively speaking) remaining on Simpsons' pegs. We hurriedly came to an arrangement to wear The Coat on alternate days, and it did enable us to play patch-as-patch-can when they got ragged.

The Messrs Morley and Rees had installed themselves in a flat in Westwood Village, which was then a tiny suburb of Beverly Hills, and had taken a jolly nice little one for me almost next door. We had a fairly eccentric Filipino servant who cooked dreamily beautiful great rice dishes and gave notice once a week. He was called Sammy and remained in our employment throughout our stay. The film had apparently not even started, and after the first day we didn't go near the studio for a bit. I had lunch there and got enough thrills to

"I Know the Face, but . . ."

last me for quite a time. At the centre table in the M.G.M. Commissary were the Messrs Gable, Tracy, Powell, a lot of Barrymores and the Mesdames Lamarr, Loy and Macdonald, and as Robert had been given Garbo's old dressing-room, I was able to bask on the famous lavatory seat to my heart's content.

In the afternoon, wandering round the huge M.G.M. Empire with my agent, I ran into a tall lanky gent with a fairly extensive vocabulary, who ended a long monologue to what turned out to be *our* agent, with a telling phrase addressed to me: "Oh, they've got you in the prison now, have they?" After he'd gone I asked my *agent-provocateur* who he was. "That's Noel Langley," he replied. "I don't think he likes it here." Like it he didn't in those days, we discovered, and made no bones about it. He was cursing a good deal at having to write scripts for Macdonald and Eddy, wrote smashing ones for *The Wizard of Oz* and *Maytime*, and with his ravishing South African wife made splendid company and handed out a lot of laughs. We were to be associated on and off for many years, though "off" was the more frequent association. After my day in the Studio I was told to relax for a bit, and so we settled down for a good many games of Monopoly (the American version with Park Avenue instead of Park Lane). We changed later to a snobby game called "High Society", the aim of which was to collect as many Social Points as possible. One could get houses in Florida, yachts, polo ponies and a camp in the Adirondacks (whatever that could be), but you lost a lot of Social points if your daughter married a bogus Count, the chauffeur or, I imagine, a camp in the Adirondacks.

We didn't play these games entirely by ourselves because, apart from the Langleys, we got to know other ex-patriates like ourselves. The literary critic of the *Observer*, John Davenport, was an amusing companion who was almost as bad a loser at Monopoly as Robert and me and, I regret to report, once upset the board ON PURPOSE.—Oh dear, I hope he's not

Two Ambitions Quenched in Two Years

going to review this book. [Thinks.] No, he only does fiction, so I'm safe.—Then there was Mary Morris, a young actress with beautiful eyes and great integrity, who came out on an idiot's contract of 75 dollars a week or thereabouts, which made living pretty difficult. The Studios could not think what to do with her, as she conformed not at all to any preconceived idea of a Film Actress, and used to test her bi-weekly in improbable costumes. One would meet her on a Monday wandering gloomily round the lot dressed as a French Courtesan at the court of Louis the something, and on the Thursday she'd be portraying a very blacked-up servant from the deep, deep South. As she also had to attend acting classes and the gymnasium, she got very unhappy indeed and eventually got her release, which resulted in an enormous personal success for her in a film called *Prison Without Bars* made in England. She did ask to be routed back from Hollywood via Siberia, which shook the Travel Department a bit.

But that was all much later, and anyhow the Metro-Goldwyn-Mayer set-up was so wrapt in mystery, intrigue and curious carryings-on that one never quite knew where one was. *Marie Antoinette* was to pass through many hands. When I first arrived out there a gentleman called Sydney Franklin, who had done several years' research on the subject, was supposed to direct it, but I think he wanted to spend rather a long time on it which didn't quite fit in with a sudden economy campaign at the studio, so the job was switched to "Woody" Van Dyke, the splendid director of *The Thin Man* series who, I am pretty sure, thought a Dauphin was a large fish. Anyhow, Mr Franklin, who had soaked himself in Versailles lore, was carried away to a nursing-home and that was that.

Mr Hunt Stromberg was the producer, and I was summoned to his office quite early on and told of many startling future plans for me, but the immediate ones concerned my learning the American tongue in order to play the French blacksmith.

"I Know the Face, but . . ."

I had an hour every day with a nice lady who turned out to be of Swedish extraction, but she made me promise not to tell. I never asked why I had to speak American, but in a way I was relieved, as lines like "Now you're sore at me" (addressed to Louis XVI of France) are not easy to say in any other language. Actually I did make the error of complaining about this very line, which resulted in a midget script conference and a new line: "Now you're mad at me."

Depicting the title role was Miss Norma Shearer, whose comeback this was to be. I believe at that time she owned 51 per cent of the shares of M.G.M. (bequeathed by her late husband Irving Thalberg), so I watched with fascination to see how she was treated. I found her enchanting and was delighted by the string quartette that she had on the set between "takes". I was also enormously impressed by her technique, though I fear she was very unhappy in her role. Others in the cast were Tyrone Power, John Barrymore, Gladys George, Joseph Schildkraut and Robert Morley. Robert was meant to support her but he didn't really. He just walked away with the film, a remarkable achievement for an actor whose only previous experience of the Bioscope was being sacked from *Under the Red Robe* at Denham Studios, England. It was an astonishing début, and his method of acting foxed the Hollywood habitués considerably.

Most of my scenes were with him and were not directed by Van Dyke who had to deal with all the Shearer scenes. But by this time, looking down their lists, M.G.M. had discovered that they had Julien Duvivier, the great French director under contract and doing damn all. He had been brought over to remake *Pepé Le Moko* which was eventually done catastrophically by another studio. So poor M. Duvivier directed crowd and odd scenes in *Marie and Toilette* as Robert now called it. He seemed fairly dispirited and with reason.

I did two days' work in the first two months, and was exhausted when it came to the big revolutionary scenes in Ver-

Two Ambitions Quenched in Two Years

sailles where the mob were to break in. We had been warned that there was going to be plenty of action, but I was a bit alarmed by the number of nurses in attendance. I later discovered that the Palace Guards had signed away their persons for bags of gold, or rather the stunt men playing the Palace Guards had. Robert and I were fairly windy and not looking forward to this sequence at all. I suddenly noticed among the crowd a large gentleman dressed exactly like me. I immediately suspected, frankly not without cause, that I had been replaced in the role of Gamin without being myself advised of the change. I went up to him and exchanged the following bizarre intercourse:

"Good morning," I said.

"Morning," he replied civilly.

"Got a good part?" I inquired cautiously.

"Doing the dangerous bits for you."

I was nonplussed.

"Do you do a lot of this kind of work?" I asked.

"Yeah," he said. "I was one of the apes in *Tarzan*."

This was a real conversation-stopper and I edged away. Later on, when I was bruised all over and had broken a bone in my elbow, I meant to ask him how he had fared; but I never saw him again. Perhaps he was a mirage. The mob were pretty tough, and we all came in for some rough handling. There was also a horrid scene when I was stabbed in the back by Barry Fitzgerald. In order to make this frightfully convincing, I was given small bags of chocolate sauce to bite on at the crucial moment, so that it spurted attractively out of my trap. We had just the 28 takes on this one, and I didn't eat chocolates for 28 months at least. The monotony of the scene and the unpleasantness of treading on a chocolate-caked carpet brought on an intense nausea, not helped by a too realistic copy of Miss Anita Louise's head (she was playing the Princesse de Lamballe) whizzing past the fairly French windows on a pike.

"I Know the Face, but . . ."

At the end of this sequence I was told I would not be needed for some time, so that I could settle down and get accustomed to life in Hollywood. This was a disheartening period and I could find no reality of any sort in the surroundings. Everyone there seemed at this time to be only interested in the film industry, and the newspapers were exclusively devoted to film news and it was frightening to see how far this self-abuse was carried. I read in one paper that "Peter Bull, the hefty British actor, is disappointed at the size of the swimming-pools in Hollywood", which item of absorbing significance was only one in a series of inanities about me.

Luckily Robert and I, being in the character-actor bracket, were not steam-rollered into a phoney romance to appease the fans and newshawks; but one young British actor of our acquaintance was. He was in those days a shy young normal gent who loved his mother, his pipe, and his Tyrolean hats, but a few days after his arrival he was instructed by his publicity department that he must be seen "squiring a dame" or everyone would think he was "queer". (Don't see *Glossary*.) He muttered something about not having the money, but they said they would look after that and detailed one of their contract ladies off to be "squired" by him. He was given the money, had a table reserved for him at a smart restaurant and was photographed continuously during the evening; but he was totally unprepared for the huge display in the Los Angeles newspapers the next day. As it had been the first occasion on which he had even seen the lady, he was astonished to find the headlines read: "David Roberts, new British heart-throb, finds romance. Ex-manicurist film star to wed import."

He remonstrated with his studio a bit because he thought his mother might not be best pleased, so they published a denial of the "engagement"; but a few weeks later it all happened again, and Robert and I very rarely saw him after this, as he

Two Ambitions Quenched in Two Years

was continuously out convincing the thirsting public that he was a Don Juan of the first water.

As no one bothered to make us Don Juans we got pretty bored, and the games of chance as played in the home were getting more and more acrimonious, so we took to driving down to town and going into a sports shop where we twiddled a roulette wheel at fifty dollars a whack, which shook Llewellyn Rees so much that he confiscated our pocket-money and kept us very short indeed. We went to the cinema a bit, and they used to have "sneak pre-views" in our local cinema. One night we wandered down there, and there seemed to be a considerable *brouhaha* in progress. A new film from our own studio was to be shown that evening and we were recognised by one of our pressmen and asked to say a few words into the mike to the listening millions. We were delighted to do so, and after delivering some sparkling dialogue we adjourned to the box-office, where we had the humiliating experience of being refused admission for the silly reason that no one had provided us with tickets. So back to Monopoly in the sanctity of the home.

The rainy season was quite funny. As California refuses to admit that it can rain much there, there are the minimum of gutters and drains to get rid of the stuff when it arrives. We had several days of cloudbursts and driving rain, and there were consequently floods and even the studios were under water. Hysterical voices on the radio told us to stay in our homes (more Monopoly) and that some Great Dam was coming unstuck, but we heeded not and waded out in order to see the dinghies and other craft that enterprising persons were sailing up and down Hollywood Boulevard.

The weeks rolled by, and we found ourselves getting more and more bored and grumpy with the inactivity, and suddenly Robert was told that he would not be needed for about ten days. This meant that I would not either, so we tootled off

"I Know the Face, but . . ."

(driven by Llewellyn) on a Round Trip of the West Coast of America. We took in the Grand Canyon (already described by some more picturesque writer than I), Boulder Dam (ditto), and Las Vegas, which in those days was a fairly tatty gambling city which Robert and I took to very kindly. The previous day to our arrival in Las V. we had spent in Salt Lake City on a Sunday which had coincided with my twenty-seventh birthday. It was quite the gloomiest birthday I had ever spent, as Salt Lake City on Sunday makes Sheffield on Sunday seem like Sodom and Gomorrah, as you cannot, or could not, obtain any drink, hot food, or indeed hot tea, as anything of this calibre apparently excites a Mormon's lustful appetite. Robert did ask me what I wanted as a birthday present, and I said to get the hell out of Salt Lake C. as quick as poss., and that's how, children, we landed up in the wicked town of Las Vegas.

From here we adjourned to Reno, "the greatest little town in the world", as is boastfully quoted on banners hanging over the streets. We were intrigued by the fruit-machines which even found their way into emporiums like boot shops, and the lists of available co-respondents with physical characteristics which were supplied in the hotels for would-be divorcers. Most of the cowboys seemed to be wearing a full film make-up, but it may have been my imagination. It wasn't, however, my imagination when I tell you that in the dear little Red-Light district all the cubicles had the names of the ladies on the outside and the whole thing looked like a rather large Dollies' Hairdressing Salon.

We spent most of our time in Reno at the fruit-machines, and Llewellyn cut down our pocket-money to just the five dollars a day in this town. This led to some pretty unpleasant scenes. We both used to wait till the other had spent all his nickels on one machine and then try and cash in on his ill-luck. I regret to say that on one occasion Robert said he would take away the rights of *Goodness, How Sad!* from me if I didn't lend

Two Ambitions Quenched in Two Years

him a nickel. I wouldn't and didn't, and got the jackpot, to Robert's fury, but he didn't keep to his threat.

On to San Francisco, which we found wildly attractive and stimulating. Can't remember what we did except be impressed by the new beauty and freshness of it all and be amused by our visits to the Chinese theatre which was conducted in a fairly unorthodox fashion. It was like the Windmill Theatre in that there was always something going on, no intervals and a great deal of coming and going. The plays were interminable and the audience either watched, read newspapers, ate their luncheon, or discussed life.

But our time was up and we journey sadly back to Los Angeles. Nothing had changed there, and I realised that I had now saved enough money to have a bash at putting on *Goodness, How Sad!* in London. Later on there was to be a headline in the *Daily Express* which read: "FOUR DAYS IN FILM PUTS ON WEST-END PLAY", a statement which was technically correct but did not best please my ex-employers. But the fact remains that I was still being kept in Hollywood, albeit on full salary, with no likelihood of ever working again. They kept burbling about possible re-takes, but as they had never taken very much (of me) in the first place, it seemed a fantasy. Just as I had made up my mind to lie back and become one of Hollywood's Forgotten Men, they told me I could go. I decided to travel across America in a puff-puff, and took a ticket on the most glamorous puff-puff in the U.S., called the Super-Chief. Llewellyn came to see me off, and Robert, to my surprise, arrived just as the guard was waving the train out of the station. I had last seen him going to the studio to work but he told me that he'd been sent to inform me that I would after all be needed for re-takes.

I was almost taken in by his performance, but wisely decided to risk it and spent a pretty boring four days getting across America. I had a night in New York at the end of it, which I spent viewing Thornton Wilder's enchanting play *Our*

"I Know the Face, but . . ."

Town. The next day I sailed in the *Aquitania* for England, in which ship I of course won the table-tennis championship. I was horrified, though, to discover that the cup presented by the British ship does not respond to Silver-Dip (Advt.), whereas its French comrade does. Still, I am the only actor in the world to have won the Blue Riband of the Atlantic for Ping-Pong. So there!

I suppose it's out of character for me to end a chapter in a blaze of glory, so I'd better insert my postscript now and not put it in "Addenda". I was cut clean out of the Metro-Goldwyn-Mayer Production of *Marie Antoinette*, but I did get my shoulders into one of the stills outside the Empire Cinema, the result of six months well and usefully spent.

Chapter III

A SLIGHT CASE OF MISMANAGEMENT

BACK in London I set about going into management with *Good ness, How Sad!* Before Robert and I left for Hollywood we had exhausted every Avenue of Possibility and had been nowhere near able to get into the Shaftesbury one. In fact, we had been driven to considering seriously such unlikely theatres as the Little Theatre and the Lyric, Hammersmith. The former used to be perched precariously behind the Tivoli Cinema, though now both places of entertainment have disappeared, and so perhaps I had better describe it as a hundred yards due south of the Adelphi. Anyhow, we were offered the theatre for £40 a week, which may seem to you a more than reasonable rent for a West-end theatre, but not when I tell you that at this period the whole of the street outside the Little was cut off from traffic owing to demolition of property. It would have involved our patrons walking quite a way, to say nothing of the artistes, and although it was a dear little theatre in its heyday it was a bit off the beaten track; though I suppose we could have advertised it as being very much on the beaten track, as the noise from the electric drills would have deafened audience and actors alike.

The Lyric Theatre, Hammersmith, was offered to us at an even more reasonable rent (£20 a week), but it seemed a wildly unsuitable home for a little comedy and at that time there was no fixed policy, and pilgrims to Hammersmith received anything from saucy nude revues to marionettes speaking Finnish. We had dallied with the Whitehall, but the gentleman who bartered with us really did expect too much money, and although there had been a week-end when we had decided to

"I Know the Face, but . . ."

blow the expense and present the play there with Jessica Tandy and Esmond Knight in the leading roles, our courage forsook us at the last moment.

At this time we had very limited capital and I had been unable to raise any more. One of the disadvantages of the poor going into management is that they have to ask people for money and I am not at all good at this. It was the same problem when I was an advertising canvasser, simply because I have never had the confidence to convince would-be investors that they would even get their money back, much less make a small fortune. However, with my pockets bulging with American dollars, I felt quite differently on my return from Hollywood.

I formed myself into a limited liability company, called for some obscure reason, Peter Bull Ltd. It is, I think, one of the few businesses extant which have actually held an Annual General Meeting in the sea. It was terribly hot at the time and seemed the best place. Having read company law, I was determined on one occasion to hold an A.G.M. in a lift; I had gathered that it would have to be stationary the whole time in order to follow correct procedure, but some silly ass kept on wanting to use the damned thing just as the Sec. was reading the minutes.

The extraordinary thing about the affairs of Peter Bull Ltd. is, that though we started off merry as grigs with £2,000 in the bank, since then we never seem to have more than 16s 3d. and I always have to pop something in when "Charges" are due. It's worrying because, although I have lost my all twice in management or mismanagement, I am still fascinated by it and the urge might seize me again at any moment and 16s. 3d. is not really sufficient to put on a distinguished production, even if the entertainment-tax burden has been raised. I suppose at a pinch we could do *Waiting for Godot*, which only needs a bare stage and a tree which has no leaves, but that play always leads to unpleasantness, as you will see later on.

A Slight Case of Mismanagement

Peter Bull Ltd. started off by being quite a family party. The shareholders (or debenture-holders as they were saucily called) were my brother Anthony, Robert Morley, Hugh Sinclair, Mr Hayes-Hunter (the author's agent), Gerald Savory (kindness induced by the success of *George and Margaret*), a friend of Frith Banbury (called, I think, Alan Roger) and Mrs Gordon Latta who had been with me in *Escape Me Never*. I put in slightly more than anyone else in order to inspire a bit of faith.

While the company was being formed, Robert Morley disappeared to New York to repeat his triumph in *Oscar Wilde*, which was just as well, as I don't think he would have enjoyed my subsequent machinations to keep all our heads above water. He did, however, help very greatly with the casting and above all persuade Tyrone Guthrie to direct the piece.

Available theatres were still pretty scarce in spite of the damping effect of the Munich crisis, but by a stroke of luck I was able to secure the Vaudeville Theatre owing to a rather macabre state of affairs. A couple of young men from Yorkshire called Schofield had taken a lease of the theatre and, flushed with enthusiasm, had announced that the Vaudeville would be "The House of Comedy". As an opening attraction they put on a play by Val Gielgud, starring the late Ronald Squire, but the piece did not "catch the public fancy" and closed in a very short time. They were caught with no follow-up and inserted a revival of *Ghosts* with Marie Ney, which was highly praised but did not quite fit in with the theatre's new policy.

As a result, when I made my bid they were not unpleased to consider a proposition. I got it fairly cheaply (£150 a week and four weeks' rent in advance) and then could go ahead with contracts, etc. The nucleus of the Perranporth production was to be preserved intact, and Roger Furse was to reproduce his superb dingy-digs set. Of the original company Judith Furse and Frith Banbury were to play their original roles, and as the

"I Know the Face, but . . ."

parts had been written for them they could not have been bettered. Pauline Letts, who had created the part of Carol the young actress round whom the play revolved, was no longer available, as by this time she was a wife and mother and showing a zest for domesticity and bringing up enchanting children which was to play havoc with her stage career. I am happy to report that she is back in harness now that domestic demands have eased. In her place we engaged a young girl called Jill Furse (a cousin of Roger and Judith). She was an actress of immense sensitivity and appeal who died at the beginning of the war. Her engagement in the piece made the Furse element so strong that one critic was to head his notice: "Goodness, How Furse!"

I martyred myself by NOT again playing Herr Angst, the gentleman with the performing seals, an act of sacrifice, as I adored the part but thought it wiser not to run the risk of making a muck of both my managerial and Thespian careers in "one foul sweep", as my mother has been heard to say. The late Arthur Hambling played the part superbly and Kathleen Boutall was enormously funny as his wife, dressed at one stage of the play in a little girl's sailor-suit. To play the important part of Mrs Priskin, the frightening landlady, we got Mary Merrall, who had rarely played comedy before and who started a new career for herself as the result of her big success.

But the most serious problem was who should play Robert Maine, the film star with whom the young actress falls in love. A lot of stars would not touch it because the part did not appear in the last scene and anyhow required a certain amount of unselfishness, and we were incredibly lucky to persuade Hugh Sinclair, then on the crest of a wave as a leading-man in films and the theatre, to play it. He contributed a charming and valuable performance, and by his experience and skill was able to help the younger members of the cast. He is always wonderfully unselfish where young people are concerned, and

A Slight Case of Mismanagement

few people who saw *Claudia* will forget the support he lent to Pamela Brown in her first starring part.

For the remainder of the set-up I was in safe and friendly hands. Margaret Fraser, a tower of strength from Perranporth, was to help the stage management, and Llewellyn Rees was to be my manager and steer me through innumerable nasty moments. It is entirely due to Mr Rees that I was not submerged in debt and disaster. In charge of publicity was a very original lady called Mrs Peggy Laing, who also handled the Windmill Theatre, assisted by a young lady of immense *joie de vivre* called Sheila Van Damm. Their method with press people was fairly unorthodox and, in Peggy's case, usually consisted of phrases like: "There's a ghastly little play coming on which I don't suppose you want to do anything about" or "Aren't these photographs dreary? You can't possibly want to use them": an approach which was so original that she practically always got what she wanted.

And there we were, all ready to go. After paying the rent for four weeks, I sat back and quite frankly enjoyed the whole thing. Rehearsals went more than smoothly and there were no rows and no temperaments. I was a little surprised that there was no advance booking, but the first night looked healthy. I got the curtain up for £1,200, which left £800 for emergencies, of which there were to be plenty. But everyone seemed to wish us well and "What's On" published a picture of me affirming that I was "the youngest manager in London". I let the capable box-office gentleman deal with the first-night applications and put everyone in their place. I did manage to persuade Elisabeth Bergner to come in a box, no mean achievement, as she loathed publicity or social functions of any sort. I left some flowers and a few indoor games in the box, in case she and Margaret Kennedy, who accompanied her, got bored. In other boxes the Furse parents (Sir William and Lady) faced the Bull parent (Lady) across the theatre and I popped assorted

"I Know the Face, but . . ."

Bulls in other boxes. Dotted all over the house were a vast assortment of friends and well-wishers from Perranporth and I had no qualms at all until my white stiff shirt refused to co-operate, broke the studs and burst open to expose most of my torso, and I had to spend the rest of the evening with a scarf round my neck, which certainly didn't qualify me for the role of "London's best-dressed manager". Luckily this occurred after being photographed with Miss Bergner arriving at the theatre and, as usual, being described as "Peter Ball" in one of the papers the next day.

Anyhow this was only a small fly in the ointment that evening, as the play went extremely well and even better than one had dared to hope. At the end there were cheers, and the reception was so enthusiastic that Hugh made a speech of thanks and told the audience that he would cable the author immediately, informing him of their delightful reaction. Later the most famous critic of the day, the late Mr James Agate, told Hugh to include his name in the cable, which sent all our spirits sky-high. This was at a party given in Roger Furse's studio after the first night, where we all adjourned and celebrated the evening in riotous fashion.

I was up at dawn to get the papers and found that they were unanimous in their approval, though several commented unfavourably on the title which still seems to me the perfect one for this play. But the general tone of the notices was very enthusiastic and I could easily see that we had our pick of quotable bits to display all over London.

>"Gladness, How Good" (*Daily Sketch*).
>"Gladdens the heart" (*Daily Express*).
>"Delightful Evening's Entertainment" (*Daily Mail*).

And the "Sundays" were to prove even better for advertising purposes.

A Slight Case of Mismanagement

"Another *French Without Tears* (*Sunday Express*).
"One long laugh" (*Sunday Pictorial*).
"One of the most entertaining plays for months"
(*Sunday Dispatch*).

But £28 5s. 8d. did not seem an adequate reward, and this is the figure to which we played on the second night. On the other hand my mother, a shrewd critic, had made two rather pertinent observations on the phone that morning.

"I enjoyed it very much, dear," she said, "but it's a pity that Jill Furse wears such dowdy clothes and there are no changes of scene. The digs are a bit depressing."

It was no good assuring her that repertory actresses do have to wear dowdy clothes and keep their best for the stage and that "digs" are depressing. It is just that the ordinary audience believe that the whole of the stage must be tinged with glamour and very few of them can even imagine what life in the lower registers of the profession really means.

However, we cheered up at the thought of what James Agate was going to say on Sunday, and as a large section of the public followed his advice implicitly, we hung on to our hats. We went up seven pounds on the Thursday and Friday nights and got into three figures for the Saturday—but only just. Even with the first night we had only played to £368 on the six performances.

You can imagine our disappointment when we tore through the theatre columns of the *Sunday Times* and found that Mr Agate had dismissed *Goodness, How Sad!* more than lightly, describing it as a "pretty minoperative" play, which was not exactly calculated to send the customers helter-skelter down the Strand. But it was the space that he devoted to his notice which was so humiliating. There were less than a dozen lines in all, culminating in the cast list, headed by the phrase: "the piece was acted for all it's worth by"; and though this did not

"I Know the Face, but..."

lead to any jealousy on the part of the artistes, it was a tremendous let-down. None of us would have minded if he had not gone so far in his praise verbally, after the first performance.

The next week (the first full one) we played to £454, which meant a loss of £200. In actual fact we should have been sitting pretty, as the get-out was only £663 a week, but four losing weeks like this would put paid to the reserves of Peter Bull Ltd.; it was doubly infuriating, as everyone in the theatre world was convinced that we had a big success on our hands and did not even bother to ask for free seats. The irony was that we had to fill the theatre every night with people recruited from any profession other than our own, to foster this illusion. It has always been a mystery to me how a box-office can suddenly muster a theatreful of willing patrons at short notice, particularly for a real flop or a play that has had appalling notices. The Vaudeville crew were really miraculous at this, and many a time I heard the manager coo down the phone and ask for "twenty well-dressed pairs". And my goodness! the goods were supplied just as ordered. Later on I used to get my friends to "dress" the boxes, if distinguished visitors were expected, and often poor Miss Pamela Brown has had to sit there, dangling a bejewelled hand over the ledge.

After we had lost over £200 on each of the two successive weeks, it was obvious that drastic steps would have to be taken. The takings were only just over £400 a week and the vast resources of P. Bull Ltd, were exhausted. And this was despite Robert Morley forgoing his royalties and Hugh Sinclair (the only remotely well-paid member of the company) popping in his cheques very belatedly. First I went to the brothers Schofield and told them I could not continue to present the play at their theatre under these circumstances. They agreed generously to let me have it at greatly reduced rent (£60 a week, in fact, though with a large increase in percentage over a certain takings' figure), and I had then to go to the cast and

A Slight Case of Mismanagement

ask them to accept cuts in their already pretty parlous salaries. They were magnanimous and co-operative, and as a result of these negotiations I was able to get the "get-out" figure down to £500 a week. Nowadays it would cost £1,200 to keep the simplest small cast one-set play operating:

I then went on an all-out campaign to bully people into coming to see the play. Friends, actors and relatives were given thousands of throwaways eulogising the piece, to leave about in buses, tubes and taxis. Restaurants were flooded with the damned things and Miss Valerie Taylor (Hugh Sinclair's wife at the time) was caught by her manager (Mr Beaumont of H. M. Tennent) distributing handbills to the enormous queues wanting to see her in *Call It A Day*. Mr Beaumont, justifiably, I think, asked her to desist.

I rang up James Agate bravely and was dismissed with a flea in my ear, when he said he could not return to a play he had already reviewed, but the late Sydney Carroll sprung to our assistance. He was then the theatrical correspondent of the *Daily Telegraph* and devoted a long article to one particular play every Thursday. In response to my appeal he picked out *Goodness, How Sad!* which had an immediate though miniscule effect on the box-office. We rose to slightly below £500 on the following week. But until Christmas we never had a profit-making week, which was maddening, as those who came were very appreciative and even the great Charles B. Cochran wrote me an ecstatic letter which I had photostated and put outside the front of the theatre.

The curious part about it all is that I never thought of taking it off or that it would ever play to such a catastrophic week that it would plunge Peter Bull Ltd. into bankruptcy. At the end of January 1939, we got associated with that pernicious system known as "twofers", by which customers could have two seats for the price of one by presenting a card which showed that they had paid a very small sum to an organisation

"I Know the Face, but . . ."

called the Privilege Ticket Register. It was a constant embarrassment to me to watch a nice customer amble up to the box-office and buy two expensive stalls for 27s., only to be followed by a "twofer" lady who got the same thing for 13s. 6d. But it did increase the intake by a little and we were able to coast into the spring. But by March we had reached the end of our reserves, though by selling the film rights to Ealing films, we were able to put some money back into the company.

At the end of March Hugh Sinclair and Jill Furse left the cast to make a bit of money in films (and who could blame them?), and I was lucky to get Sebastian Shaw and Jenny Laird to replace them. They were excellent, and continued in the play until the run ended on May 6th, 1939, having achieved 237 performances.

The only people who did remotely well out of it financially were Guthrie, who had directed it superbly for a minute basic fee but then went on a percentage, and Roger Furse, who had designed the set for love and, I am ashamed to admit, £15 and a tiny percentage. For the company it must be said that the play made the reputations of all those actors who had none at the commencement, and the management glowed with the record of an eight months' run as a first venture.

The last week we played to a very cool £320, but, to cheer us up, dear Robert Morley, who had made less than anyone on the production, in spite of his authorship, sent us a large sum of money to have an outing on the first Monday after we had closed. So off we set to a splendid tuck-in across the road from the Stage Door at Rule's Restaurant, where a special menu (headed "In Memoriam Goodness, How Sad!") was given to us and then we all went, with our wives or whatever we had with us at the time, to see Herbert Farjeon's lovely revue *Nine Sharp* at the Little Theatre.

And that was that. I felt no remorse or bitterness about the play, as it could not be classed as a failure in the ordinary

A Slight Case of Mismanagement

sense. Both the Press and the public liked it, but as it has never done well since, either on tour or in the repertory theatres, I can only guess that it lacks popular appeal. But it will always be revived as it is a remarkably true and honest play, which provides splendid parts for actors who can for a change understand what they are talking about. It has some touching stuff, as when the young actress turns on the film star who has said he won't help them by appearing in their dying "rep":

CAROL. We listened to you and now it's our turn. We're the theatre, see! You may have forgotten what that is, but I'll remind you. It's the place where you learned your job, which cradled you, which gave you your first chance, which made an actor out of you, which sent you to Hollywood to make pictures. And just because you don't need us any more you think you can walk out on us . . . well, you can't. You've got a debt to pay, Robert Maine, and you're not going to get away without paying it! It's a big debt too. You're happy now, you're rich, you're doing what you like, you're proud of yourself. Well, everything you've got you owe to us. There wouldn't be any pictures at all if it wasn't for the theatre. The theatre, that's something bigger than anything you'll ever know in Hollywood, something that was going hundreds of years before the cinema was ever heard of, and you know and I know it will be going on thousands of years after motion pictures are dead and buried. The greatest author that ever lived once described the whole thing in five words, "All The World's a Stage".

To which the poor film star can only reply: "Have a glass of water."

And the observation throughout is so acute. Listen to the little scene where the two girls in the company are reading the eagerly awaited notice in the local paper.

CAROL. Here we are. "Amusements."

"I Know the Face, but..."

CHRISTINE. That's something, anyway.

CAROL. "Sea Lions at the Hippodrome." Why do they always put the Hippodrome before us?

CHRISTINE. Their advertisement is bigger.

CAROL. "The Repertory Company at the Opera House is presenting *When in Rome* this week. This is a smart and witty comedy well suited to the talented company. Mr Osbert Faith is convincing as the Father, while Miss Carol Sands scores heavily as Millicent. Mr Peter Thropp makes use of his rich comic opportunities and mention must be made of Miss Christine Lawford as a maid. The settings by Arthur Hardy are excellent and Mr Lambert is the popular front of the house manager."

Why do they bother to put that in each week?

CHRISTINE. Mr Lambert writes the notice himself, I imagine.

It seems to me that there in a tiny scene is reflected all the heartbreak and comedy of the theatrical profession. But I must not quote any more from this (to me) entrancing play, and I leave it with the regret that it obviously cannot be everyone's cup of tea.

Shortly after the end of the run in London, Mr Baxter Somerville, who runs the beautiful Theatre Royal in Brighton, took over the touring rights and, after a bit of a tussle about the scenery downpayment, opened a pretty disastrous tour in his own theatre. The leading parts were played by Ann Casson, Margaret Fraser, Roderick Lovell and Mary Merrall (in her original role). It was extremely well done, and Robert was able to catch his play at Oxford on his return from America. It played to under £300 on its first week, but this was riches compared to the week at the Opera House, Manchester (where you can play to £5,000 or over. *Goodness, How Sad!* gathered £172 5s. 10d., which wasn't entirely satisfactory. But even so, the returns from the Imperial Hall, Frinton-on-Sea, make sorrier

A Slight Case of Mismanagement

reading. The play opened to a not very healthy £7 11s. 3d., only touched double figures twice on the week, the receipts of which totalled £80 8s. 8d., and as this was August in a smart seaside resort, there must have been something wrong somewhere.

But it never quite died, and during the war popped up at some very surprising places, including the Coliseum Theatre, where Carol was played by Miss Sarah Churchill. By then, unfortunately, Robert and I had sold the rights or rather our share of them for a mess of pottage, as we needed the pottage at the time.

The film of the play turned out to be a grievous disappointment. Though Robert Stevenson, who directed it, had professed a great love for the play and had indeed seen it three nights in succession, the end-product bore no resemblance to the original. Not one single line was retained and not one of the stage actors was engaged for the film. The title chosen was *Return to Yesterday*, and Clive Brook and Anna Lee (then Mrs Robert Stevenson) were the stars. At the eleventh hour the director tried to persuade Robert to bring back some of the original flavour, but he wisely declined.

It was now nearly summer 1939 and full of fresh hopes and enthusiasm, a lot of us went down to Perranporth for what was to prove the last season of the Summer Theatre. I had a brand new play by Noel Langley, called *The Walrus and the Carpenter*, with which I hoped to recoup my losses, and an exceptionally strong company, which included Miss Pamela Brown, a lot of Furses and Mr Robert Morley. But on September 3rd, 1939, we had to close the theatre owing to circumstances over which we had no control, and we all ended up in some very peculiar places (see *To Sea in a Sieve* by Peter Bull).

Chapter IV

MUDDLING THROUGH AGAIN

You might have thought that after *Goodness, How Sad!* I'd think thirty-six times before embarking on a managerial venture again; but not a bit of it. I came bustling out of the Navy, clasping my gratuity not quite tightly enough to my bosom, and before you could say "Prince Littler" I was at it again. At the risk of being a bore, I must take you back to that post-war era when there was a tremendous boom in the entertainment industry and a great many people were flinging a lot of money around. I had had dreams during my Navy career of returning triumphantly to management and engaging all my closest friends to act in highly successful plays written by chums, directed by chums and designed by chums. After six years' exile it was impossible to believe that everyone was not necessarily on one's side. I realised that we were all too old to start up the Perranporth Summer Theatre again (lugging all those tables and chairs about, etc.), and I decided to try to find a straight play to put on.

There seemed to be none forthcoming, but I was suddenly approached by Noel Langley with what looked like a reasonably attractive proposition. Noel had adapted his own saucy book *Cage Me a Peacock* and gathered around him several ex-service types, some of whom had been P.O.W.s on the Burma Road. One of them was an actor I'd known before the war, called Jack Macnaughton, and another was a chartered accountant named Norman Smith. The former supplied the enthusiasm and ideas, and the latter a delightful musical score and a good deal of backing. Norman came from Halifax and had formed a producing company called, I have to admit,

Muddling through Again

West-End Quality Productions Ltd., who proposed to present the play with Peter Bull Ltd. (as usual to 16s. 3d.). There was £3,000 in the kitty and a promise of more. It was, like *Goodness, How Sad!*, to be largely on a sharing basis, and both Noel Langley and I put some money in ourselves.

It was a fairly difficult show to cast as, like most modern musicals, the parts demanded actors who were "straight" but could also sing; and as there was no chance of an immediate West-End Theatre, it was difficult to persuade a cast that an indefinite tour meant that their careers would be helped by this sort of job. Luckily a lot of talented people had just come out of the services and only wanted to be "in work". From this group I got Michael Anthony and Ronald Waters, two stalwarts of pre-war Farjeon revues, David Evans who, like Jack Macnaughton, had been in the early Gate revues, and (to play the two leading men) Ballard Berkeley, who had a splendid voice and a bravura personality, and Barry Mackay, an ex-Guards Officer who had been Jessie Matthews' leading man in several of her most successful films. He was still very handsome, though struggling with the same weight problem as his prospective management. He easily got the better of it on this score, as indeed he did about salary and billing, for which he bargained with me in the lounge of the Guards Club. (Memo. to would-be managers: Never, repeat *never*, discuss terms in the Guards Club with a member.)

But the whole enterprise depended on our choice for Althea, the slave girl who turned into a great lady, and it required an enormously attractive young woman who could sing and play high-ish comedy. We were completely stumped until somebody had a brainwave. For many years a great favourite of Variety and Radio, Phyllis Robins had recently been in a Firth Shephard revue, and physically and vocally was perfect casting for us, though she had never appeared in London in a straight show. Diminutive, talented, with a penchant for

"I Know the Face, but . . ."

Siamese cats and cooking, she arrived an hour late for the first reading, but it was quite useless worrying after she had said the first few lines. She was Althea and that was that.

Other members of the cast included the late Aubrey Dexter, Phyllis Morris and a small chorus of six charming damsels. V. difficult to choose, as they had to be good singers, dancers and actresses and receive practically no money for their pains. I wish I could say a decade later that they are now all stars but in fact most of them married and "settled down", and jolly good luck to them because they were dears and loyal and everything one could have desired.

Against all this array of talent and experience, we had unfortunately committed ourselves to a director who knew little about anything. It was the major blunder of a hazardous enterprise, but he had been splendid directing shows in the P.O.W. camp, so everyone thought it would be all right; but it wasn't and it was too late to do anything about it. To compensate for this deficiency we were lucky to get William Chappell to do the dances, and inventive and jolly patient he was too. I shall not easily forget discussing terms with him in "The Bunch of Grapes" in the Brompton Road. Billy was much in demand at the time, and I could hardly bring myself to mention the sum I was prepared to offer for his services. Finally, I took my courage and large brandy in both hands, and he sat stockstill with a glazed expression on his face. There was a frightening pause: "If," he said at last, "you were Firth Shephard or Tom Arnold, I'd walk slowly backwards out of this pub screaming the place down, but seeing it's you of course I'll do it."

It was, I'm afraid, like that all along the line. We had such a narrow margin of budget that all risks had to be shared, and everyone was to receive percentages according to their contribution. I found myself waving possible astronomical figures in front of startled faces, but Harry Foster, Miss Robins' agent, nearly fainted when I mentioned her proposed basic fee.

Muddling through Again

The unfair thing was that I could not economise on the sets and dresses, which had to look *chic* and exciting, and I had Edgar Ritchard, the painter, design these, and that side of the show turned out to be impeccable. Norman Rutherford, now assistant Head of Drama for BBC Television, was my stage director. He had had a sister-ship to mine in the war and, though that didn't necessarily qualify him for the assignment, I knew him well enough to be confident that it would ensure the minimum of chaos and the maximum of loyalty. Philip Martell was to conduct the orchestra and Norman Smith, the composer, who had also found most of the original backing, allowed himself one extravagance. This was a lady harpist who cost a pretty penny to transplant (with her instrument) from such places as Dudley to Chatham.

Finding an office had been a major problem. I decided against using my mother's sitting-room, as a long series of glamorous young ladies applying for jobs might have disturbed her and Mrs Dale's Diary. Suddenly the director of the play made one of his only useful contributions to the production. He was himself living in a rather superior doss-house at the corner of Park Lane. The building was about to be rebuilt and there were some pretty extraordinary inhabitants using it for some fairly odd purposes, but I did manage to lease a tiny office for £3 13s. 6d. per week. It had a built-in washbasin clearly visible, and it was not very impressive or satisfactory. So sinister was the entrance that I am sure half the cast (female) were certain that they were about to be pricked with hypodermics and shipped off to Rio, instead of, as it turned out, Leicester and Dudley. Also my secretary Audrey had either to stay in the loo while I conducted an interview or (worse!) listen to me making a fool of myself. But as she was a dear girl who had been a champion skater, this sort of thin ice made her feel at home.

So there we were with an office, a cast and a certain amount of money but, before going into the longish saga of our disaster,

"I Know the Face, but . . ."

I would like to paint a tiny picture of the state of the theatre around this time (1946). There was, as I have said, an enormous boom, and the most unlikely shows were attracting customers in the West End, and you could not get a theatre for love or money. The only chance of arriving in London was to have a long tour producing such astonishing financial results that the lessees of the West End would grudgingly remove a show that was slightly on the wane. I suppose, looking back on it, that I was an absolute mutt and battling against quite impossible odds, but I was certainly misled by the tales of vast profits to be made by EVERY first-class show on tour.

All I had to offer was a sophisticated musical comedy with only one name in it; and unfortunately Miss Robins had only a Variety public and reputation which did not alas! appeal to the South Coast ladies who form the backbone of the Bournemouth, Brighton and Eastbourne audiences. The phrase, "Oh she's a crooner", could often be heard outside a theatre where we were playing; it was poison to the box-office, and it wasn't till mid-week that news of her sensational performance had reached the lounges of the private hotels, and word of mouth had penetrated the longest ear-trumpet.

But at the outset I was filled with a dotty confidence and courage that bred a hope that some great mogul of the London theatre would catch *Cage Me A Peacock* on tour and insist on it being brought in immediately, to shed lustre on the Lyric, Apollo, New or Globe Theatres or even the Haymarket. I explained to the cast that the tour would only last six weeks and tried not to notice the raising of eyebrows from even the least cynical member of the company. We were to open at the Devonshire Park Theatre, Eastbourne, and proceed to Brighton (short journey, cheap fares, should have been all right). Then Cambridge, Cardiff, Bournemouth, Leicester and after that, who knew?

Rehearsals progressed calmly and fairly smoothly, though

Muddling through Again

the director was not inspiring great confidence in his cast. Noel Langley had kindly, but as it turned out later, unwisely, decided to stay away. I pottered in and out of the dusty rehearsal rooms breathing, I hoped, goodwill and confidence. I had foreseen a spot of trouble with the Lord Chamberlain over the script, parts of which, I must admit, were a bit cheeky. But he sensibly passed the whole thing except for four deletions and a splendid Command in royal red, that the line: "I have a particularly small one", must not be accompanied by any gesture. Miss Robins acceded to the request.

We were due to open at Eastbourne on Monday, May 27th, 1946, so we had a dress rehearsal on the Sunday, which was no more catastrophic than usual affairs of this sort. The only snag from my point of view was that it went on till about three in the morning, which meant the expenditure of a small fortune on double, treble, Sunday time being paid to the scenery shifters and orchestra. In most towns that we were to visit there was a resident orchestra, and we just supplied a few key-men to make the Monday night cacophony not too eardrum-breaking.

The day of the first night dawned, and I lay in bed looking at some sheets of figures and breaking out into a sweat at the immensity of my folly. But even with a feeling of doom hanging over me I gave, I hope, the impression of not having a care in the world. The first night went quite astonishingly well and boded well for the future. *Cage Me A Peacock* looked a million dollars scenically, the cast were confident and played up, and Miss Robins had a small triumph. I look back now at the log book, filled in by the meticulous stage-management, and find the following entry: "Rang up at 7.34. Curtain at 10.11. Two intervals of 11 minutes and 18 respectively (big scene change). Weather Fine. Ten Curtain calls and speech by Miss Robins."

No mention of the Eastbourne tides and no reference to the financial aspect of the affair. But the bald facts must be stated at once. We had £3,000, and it had cost £3,113 15s. 4½d. to

"I Know the Face, but . . ."

get the curtain up at 7.34 at the Devonshire Park Theatre, Eastbourne, which did not really allow for possible loss on the tour. For those who are sufficiently interested, the halfpenny belongs to the "petty cash" section. Nowadays, I imagine, the smallest musical would cost anything from £8,000 upwards, and in view of this, my expenditure was not so outrageous. My mistake lay in not increasing the capital BEFORE production.

Scenery had cost £810 12s. 0d. (there were many changes of scene and several front cloths), just beating the costumes, etc., which cost just the £809 15s. 0½d. (oh, that bloody halfpenny again!). Other pre-production costs included advance payments to producer, designer, rehearsal money and rehearsal rooms. Salaries paid before the first night came to the astonishing sum (which I know you will think I am making up) of £499 19s. 11½d., not really frightfully short, let's face it, of £500.

I was also paying myself £20 a week for putting the dashed thing on, which, however, I was soon to stop paying myself; in fact, immediately after the first night. And the same attitude was adopted by the author and composer, who were even more generous than I, in that they forwent royalties throughout the tour and even put some money into the fathomless pool.

But there were other problems than the financial one and, though the play got good notices and audiences obviously enjoyed it, there was a lot of work to be done on the production. Certain scenes were messy and unproduced, there was a general air of untidiness, and it did not take long to gather from Noel Langley that, to put it mildly, he was not best pleased with the interpretation of his work. The director left quietly and in a gentlemanly fashion for Australia, South Africa and America, roughly in that order.

Noel decided to re-produce it himself; this seemed the best and most intelligent solution, because although he is not the most placid of men, he can inspire confidence and enthusiasm

Muddling through Again

in any project to which he is dedicated. By the end of the week it was a different show, compact and stylish, but we had lost £549 14s. 0d. on the date. This figure did include the dress rehearsal, but even so was a bit frightening. One of our angels, a Mr Horace Rhodes from Halifax, stumped up a further £500 in the lounge of his hotel, and I hurriedly arranged for an overdraft of £500 at my bank. We all pressed on to the Theatre Royal, Brighton, where I hoped things would improve. They did, and we lost only £135 14s. 1½d. *that* week.

It was a strange week as throughout it I felt that the show had enormous possibilities, both financial and otherwise. Quite a lot of people came down from London, including one or two managers, and the general opinion was that "I had got something there". What I didn't have was any capital and although business went gradually up throughout the week we did not attract the sophisticated crowds that I had previously imagined thronged the Brighton boulevards. But it is a small comfort to me that every time I revisit the theatre as an actor I am greeted by one of the house-managers with a medley of the show's numbers.

Our next port of call was the Arts Theatre, Cambridge, which was wonderful for morale but terrible for the pocket, as even if we had played to absolute capacity, we should still have sustained a loss. It is a tiny theatre, and as it was May week we did nearly fill it at every perf., but £249 2s. 10d. went whistling down the drain. To counteract this, Miss Robins was the toast of the University town and, judging by the reception every night, one might have thought our troubles were over. The cast anyhow were in great heart and had what is commonly known as a ball. I was by this time, I have to confess, absolutely potty about Miss Phyllis Robins and was determined to make her the biggest musical comedy star since Miss Gertrude Lawrence. For who could resist a lady who sewed her own costumes if they needed attention, taught the chorus harmonies,

"I Know the Face, but . . ."

never stopped looking a dish, had enormous talent and improved at every performance?

It was during the Cambridge week that she pulled me into her dressing-room and told me to sit down while she put on some make-up.

"Want any money?" she asked.

"No; why?" I replied hurriedly.

"Just wondered," she said, adjusting the bun at the back of her lovely head. "Your cheque bounced last week."

I went immediately more purple in the face than is my wont. I realised that she must have presented the cheque at a bad moment when I was just about to arrange for a further overdraft.

"Mind you," said Miss Robins dreamily, "I don't mind a bit. I'll go on popping it in until it doesn't bounce, but do let me know if you want more lolly."

It was no good pretending that she was not unique among leading ladies. She was.

Looking through the log book for the Cardiff week which followed, I find that we took an enormous number of curtain calls every night, culminating in ten on the Friday, which hardly explains the loss of £282 18s. 6d. on the week. But I do remember that even the Mayor of Cardiff enjoyed it, and though on the Wednesday (quote log book) "Miss de Peyer and Miss Bevan were off in scene I" (unquote) I can't think their absence can have affected the business, particularly in view of the fact that the weather was (quote) "wet and windy" (unquote).

On to Bournemouth where I had hoped for great things. The Pavilion is huge, horrid to play in, but one can sometimes take enormous money. Here for the first and only week of the tour of *Cage Me A Peacock* we made a profit. It was only £31 11s. 2d., but the actors on their percentages did quite well for a change. Thirty pounds were not going to extricate me,

Muddling through Again

however, from the creek up which I had steered myself so firmly. There was no further backing to be obtained, and I had by now reached the end of my National Savings Certificates, gratuity and indeed entire capital. The following week we landed up in Leicester, which was catastrophic. In theory it was to be the last date of the tour and it certainly was the most unpleasant. We ended up £497 8s. 4½d. in the red. It was a desperate seven days for me, and I spent half of it trying to get some other management interested in coming in with me on practically any terms. The other half I spent trying to raise the money to pay the salaries that fell due on the Friday. My friends were quite wonderful. Frith Banbury came to lunch with me unsuspecting, and although I did, I think, pay for the meal, it cost Frith £200. Hugh Sinclair had £100 ready for me within ten minutes of my calling him on the blower. However, I got only £1 for my Naval Uniform, which I finally disposed of in Camberwell High Street, in a clothing store at the entrance of which I met a mounted policeman, who turned out to my embarrassment to have been in my Flotilla.

£301 went quite far towards the salaries and, having got an advance out of the Opera House, Leicester, I scraped through that week. But I had nowhere near enough resources to face what was coming up on the next lift. I had been approached by two wildly unsuitable theatres to take *Cage Me A Peacock* to them on the two following weeks. They were the Hippodrome, Dudley, and the Theatre Royal, Chatham. Beggars couldn't be choosers and I decided to take the risk. The Dudley house was enormous, usually had big revues visiting it, and one could play to over £4,000 on the week. We took £434 7s. 11d., which wasn't quite the same thing. It didn't help matters to hear on the bush telegraph that another actress had announced at a *soirée* that she hoped to do the play in London and that a very powerful management was securing the rights.

I went up to Dudley on the Friday and you may well wonder

"I Know the Face, but . . ."

how I managed to get the cash *that* week. By a freak of chance the Chatham Theatre had given us a guarantee of £500, which was enough security to raise the salary money for the preceding week. A heat wave was in full progress at Dudley, and it was no comfort to read in the log book: "Weather wonderful! Curtain call at the Wed. Matinée." It was all grisly and I felt sick to the stomach, but Miss P. Robins was able to dispel my despair. I went into her dressing-room with a face as long as the film of *War and Peace*, and she led me out on the balcony, kissed me, and finally opened her mouth.

"Now listen to me," she said, suddenly speaking like a Sergeant-Major, "I shall never repeat what I am about to say, but if you want to do anything about it, do it at once, and it'll make no difference to what I feel about you and the show and the beating everyone is taking. This is what you must do. If you can get the damned thing on in London with any other lady as Althea (repeat any other lady) do it, if it'll save everyone's bacon."

After that I got pretty soppy, watched the show and disappeared, more determined than ever to present Phyllis Robins in *Cage Me A Peacock* in London. In the meantime I had only eight more performances (at Chatham) in which to persuade any other managements to take a dekko. One of the reasons I had closed with the Chatham offer was that it was within spitting distance of London and therefore anyone remotely interested could slip down. I did write or phone every manager in London and quite a lot of them promised to come. I said that if they would care to take the gamble, they could have the whole production, obliterate my name from it and not pay me a penny until all production costs (theirs) had been paid off. As it turned out, only two managers bothered to come down. One brought his own whisky to consume during the show, possessed a theatre and didn't like our piece; the other didn't bring his whisky, had no theatre at the time, but liked the piece.

Muddling through Again

It is possible, of course, that some of them had visited the Theatre Royal, Chatham, previously, in which case their reluctance to repeat the experience was more explicable. It was usually the home of Nude Shows with those witty titles like *Tit-Bits of 1948*, *Fanny Get Your Fun*, *No Nudes is Bad News*, or quite simply *Up the Girls*. But a new management had taken over and the standard of entertainment offered suddenly rose. But not conditions either front or back stage. The plumbing was beyond belief and the front of the house had a strong look of the Paddington station public lavatory. Against all this it was the only theatre in Britain which had offered me a guarantee of £500, which would just get us out, even if we didn't reach that figure as "our share", with a loss of £150.

The £500 bit seemed almost too good to be true, and being by now strongly suspicious of everybody, I told my manager, Bill Raynor, to have a jolly good look at the contract. He had a jolly good look, and before you could say knife we saw breakers ahead. The Management told us that there would be no Saturday matinée. Mr Raynor pointed out that if we did not play the eight performances stipulated in the contract, it would be possible for the management to find a loophole through which they needn't pay the guarantee. We then suggested that we should play twice-nightly on the Saturday, which seemed a reasonable solution. The Management said they couldn't agree to this, as the patrons would have no public transport after the second house. This was patently nonsense, but I insisted on playing the Saturday matinée. We arrived in the town to find the bills had not included this proposed perf., so we had to have them all slipped across with a special announcement. The upshot was that we played to under £5 on the matinée but, as I pointed out to the hysterical company on the stage afterwards, they and it had saved me £500. I never found out what would have happened if we'd only played seven perfs. and it's

"I Know the Face, but . . ."

possible that the whole fantasy was a figment of my distorted imagination.

The cast coped gallantly with the appalling conditions backstage and spent a lot of the week writing outraged letters to Equity about it, and it didn't help when the ladies of the chorus saw a Chatham gentleman committing slightly more than a nuisance outside their window. We rang down on July 20th, 1946, with the 65th performance ("weather fine"), and the venture had cost £6,000, exactly double the estimated total. I think the complete financial chaos was largely due to my inefficiency and pig-headedness; I was certainly not interfered with, and only a lunatic would have gone on pouring money down the drain. I still think it was a pretty good show and did not lack distinction of a kind, but its ultimate fate in the West End (I am referring to my production, not the one that did get there) was problematical. But one thing I am sure of, and that is that Phyllis Robins would have become a musical comedy star overnight.

There was a great deal of clearing up to be done and it was not terribly gay back in the office in Park Lane, which I abandoned as soon as possible. I still had a faint hope of some miracle happening and asked the cast not to accept other engagements without consulting me. But gradually it became obvious that at the time no one else was remotely interested in presenting the *Peacock* in London, and I lapsed into a morass of self-pity, which was to last many months. During this period Noel Langley behaved impeccably and generously, and when he worked on a film called *They Made Me A Fugitive*, he managed to cram a high percentage of those connected with his previous venture into it. Ballard Berkeley, Milo Lewis (now the producer of *The Army Game* and then a young singing shepherd), and Jack Macnaughton all had parts. Phyl Robins sang, in a night-club scene, one of the numbers from our ill-fated show and I played a peculiar and extremely large stool

Muddling through Again

pigeon called "Fidgety Phil". It was rather an exciting film directed by Cavalcanti and is constantly re-shown on television.

After a great many vile months in which friends were invaluable, I did manage to pay all the debts and bills. A lot of the businesses to whom I owed money were generous enough to say that I needn't pay the whole amount, but I was pig-headed and proud, and anyhow thought it a wise step in case I ever went into management again. Quite suddenly out of the blue Noel Langley announced that his agents, Linnit and Dunfee, were willing to put *Cage Me A Peacock* on in London. I was delighted and excited until I heard the entire set-up. There was to be new music, a new designer, but above all the leading part was to be played by Miss Yolande Donlan. Although I admire the latter enormously and think her a wonderful actress, I was heartbroken for Miss Robins and washed my hands clean of the whole thing. I realise now that Noel acted for the best according to his own lights, and he had up till then behaved with intense integrity and generosity. But I lost my head yet again, had a dreadful row with him, and settled back in a permanent sulk. Apart from Ballard Berkeley, Milo Lewis and the Musical Director, Philip Martell, no one was re-engaged, and the new show opened at the Strand Theatre on June 18th, 1948, ran for a year at that theatre and subsequently the Cambridge and, I believe, never made much money. I kept severely away, but eventually West-End Quality Productions were paid a tiny percentage of Noel's royalties, after a series of threatened law suits. I kept clear of this, though I did attend the voluntary winding-up of the company's affairs in Halifax in the snow.

I sold the costumes to the Boltons Theatre for a mess of porridge, but otherwise never recovered any of my losses. Luckily by the following year I was just solvent again and in fairly regular work. I continued to see Miss Robins, who had by now unfortunately got the "legitimate" acting bug and was doing tours and plays at Windsor, which was handy for her bungalow

"I Know the Face, but..."

on Ham Island, where she cooked sumptuous meals, carried out a strange racing system and drove pretty terrifyingly round the countryside. Later she went to Australia and had a fabulous success back in Variety, but I fancy this depressed her and she married a Mr Mark Hickman and retired to Devon, where she first helped him run a farm and then an hotel. I personally will always believe that she's a great loss to the theatre, which sadly needs radiant personalities on the musical side.

I carried on a half-hearted feud with Noel Langley for several years and the flames were fanned by a series of slightly unhappy coincidences. The first was when I discovered that a play of his called *Little Lambs Eat Ivy*, which was to run for a year or so at the Ambassadors, turned out to be *The Walrus and the Carpenter*, the first performance of which I had presented at Perranporth in 1939. I had, I do realise, no claim of any sort, but it would have been nice to have had some acknowledgement on the programme and one or two seats for the second night. A few years later another play of his set off on a tour and never reached London. I only discovered about my connection with it by chance, lunching with one of the actresses rehearsing in it. I took a look at a script.

"What's this, dear?" I asked.

"A Noel Langley play," said Miss Ann Walford.

"Goodness!" I said, and took a dekko at the list of characters.

It didn't take me more than a few seconds to realise that the piece was in fact *Friendly Relations* which we had done at Perranporth in 1938. This time it was being directed by James Donald and starring Kathleen Harrison and James Hayter.

"Pamela Brown found the part very difficult. Yours, I mean," I said to Miss Walford, whose pretty eyes nearly popped out of her head. "Do ask Mr Donald if he wants any help with the production."

None of this helped the Langley-Bull *impasse*, and more letters singed their way through letter-boxes. A few months later I

Muddling through Again

went to have drinks with a lady who lived in Egerton Crescent. As I came into the room she buttonholed me and drew me aside, and asked: "Do you know Noel Langley?" I turned and found myself face to face with him, and we roared with laughter and made it up in seven seconds dead, which all goes to prove something or other about personal contact.

But out of the shambles of *Cage Me A Peacock* one invaluable thing happened, and that was my association with the composer Norman Smith, who went quietly back to his accountancy, with, I suspect, a bit of his heart bruised. It's again a pity, because his music was enchanting, but if he'd had a great success with it, I think he would probably have stopped being an accountant, and in that case would not have had the dubious pleasure of looking after both Peter Bull and Peter Bull Ltd., to say nothing of the other cattle he has littering his lovely farm in Yorkshire.

Chapter v

I HAVE MY CHANCE (AND MISS IT)

THERE is a famous theatrical anecdote related of the late Lilian Baylis and a wretched actor who was sent on at a moment's notice to play Hamlet (Full Length version) at the Old Vic. Having stumbled through the role, and on his knees with gratitude at having got through it at all, he fell sweating into the arms of Miss Baylis, who was waiting for him to come off the stage. "Well, you've 'ad your chance," she said grimly, "and missed it."

I feel rather the same about an unfortunate excursion of mine into the realms of the Bioscope in the summer of 1947 and onwards. I had had a bad year, what with getting the s—k [1] at Stratford and still being in debt owing to *Cage Me A Peacock*, and was anxious to lay my hands on anything that brought in the doubloons. I was suddenly summoned to Ealing Film Studios for a small part in a film about to be shot there dealing with the Affaire Koenigsmark. Thither I hied, and was making my way to the casting office when I ran into Mr Basil Dearden who was to direct the film. He remarked that he did not know I was out of the Navy, let alone hoping to be in his film. But suddenly a strange look came into his face and he told me not to leave the building until I had seen him again.

So I carried on with my normal business and saw the Casting Director, Roger Ould, who was courteous and kind until interrupted by a phone call, during which he stared at me as if I was a Thing from Outer Space. I wondered if I'd got leprosy or some obscure plague, but he put the instrument down and announced that the director and producer of the film wished to see me. I

[1] Details of s—k in Chapter viii.

I Have My Chance (and Miss It)

was ushered into the Art Department (the producer, Michael Relph, also designed the miraculous sets and costumes), and after a brief exchange of pleasantries, Mr Relph looked me over, hummed and hahed, and told me that that very afternoon one of the leading parts in their projected film had become, as they say in the columns of *The Stage*, unexpectedly vacant. Was I prepared to make a Test for the role?

Was I not!!!!

The character was George-Louis of Hanover (subsequently George I of England), the film was entitled *Saraband For Dead Lovers*, after the book by Helen Simpson, and the other leading parts were to be played by Stewart Granger, Françoise Rosay, Flora Robson, Frederick Valk and Joan Greenwood. It was to be made in Technicolor and was to take several months.

I travelled back in the Tube from Ealing suspended on air, and reported a few days later and made an elaborate test, dressed largely in Dennis Price's boots and something as usual that had been worn by Robert Morley. At the end of a gruelling day Mr Dearden, who had been kindness and patience themselves, informed me that the part was as good as mine and that I'd be hearing from them in a few days after everyone concerned had viewed the test. I waited for two weeks and, unable to contain myself in London, asked for permission to leave for Cornwall. They said it was all right, but that I must be prepared to return at a moment's notice. I left for the West Country, happily unaware that they were stuffing the faces of all the character actors in town, testing them in the hope that they could (as one says in poker) "improve". After I had landed the part, I met at least half a dozen actors who had expected to get it.

So there I was, down at Mevagissey, trying to and indeed succeeding in forgetting the whole business while I stayed with one of my ex-shipmates, Ken Shearwood. After a year of strenuous fishing with the local fleet, he was running a curi-

"I Know the Face, but..."

ously irregular tripper-ship service to neighbouring seaside resorts, and I was roped in mainly to collect the fares, which he disliked doing, and to keep the customers occupied while he fiddled with the engines of the fairly good ship *Coral*. As there were no lifeboats supplied and his mechanical knowledge was practically *nil*, I had to do some pretty strenuous overacting in order that alarm and despondency didn't spread.

Actually the passengers were usually complacent and happily unaware of the dangers they were facing, but there was every now and again an Incident. Sometimes the boat was unable to get right into the jetty at low tide, and Ken carried the ladies in his waders (I mean, he was wearing the waders) to the shore, but he once or twice dropped them with a resounding plop in the far from deep blue sea. And there was a fairly acrimonious occasion on which we were running a trip to St Mawes. It was an expensive one for the customers (15s. a head) and it was a foggy day. Twice we narrowly missed some rocks, and a rather shrewd gent said as we airily neared what looked like the French Coast: "Didn't know we were going to Dieppe."

"We aren't, sir," I replied coldly, "I went there six years ago on a raid and it wasn't at all nice." The sarcasm rode over his head, and I was so horrified by my showing-off and bad taste that I slunk into what was amusingly referred to as "the stern sheets", but on this occasion consisted of tar and Ken's Labrador, Kim.

I emerged to collect the money and dish out a good deal of misinformation. I had been to St Mawes several times when at Perranporth, and vaguely remembered its environs. I urged the tourists to look at the lovely old church of St Just in Roseland. I pointed out that it was only half a mile away and well worth a visit.

The customers left the ship and Mr and Mrs Shearwood and I (the crew) hastened to have a rather expensive lunch at the

I Have My Chance (and Miss It)

best hotel in St Mawes. After stuffing ourselves silly and washing it down with some dark red liquid, we thought we'd visit that lovely old church of St Just. On inquiry we found that it was at least four miles away even for a crow, and looking out of the window we found that the rain was coming down in buckets. We realised we'd have to face our patrons anyhow for the return trip and hired a taxi. A Rolls-Royce arrived and carted us off. On the way we passed some of the bedraggled ladies and gentlemen who formed our ship's complement, and when we eventually regained our ship there was considerable coldness, not to mention dampness, afoot.

You may think that all this has nothing to do with being in a film with Stewart Granger, and how right you are! But I thought I'd like to show you that I'm not completely one-track-minded and can concentrate on other things; but there I was in deepest Cornwall and had almost given up hope of ever appearing in any entertainment again, let alone in glorious Technicolor, when suddenly a telegram arrived from the Ealing casting director which read: "Congratulations—you have the part. Can you write? OULD." I sent back a telegram saying, "Thanks ever so. Yes." And it wasn't until several weeks later that I learnt to my cost that what he meant was "Can you ride?"

Anyhow, I beetled back to London, and apart from throwing the make-up department into a frenzy by being as black as a berry, everyone was delightful and appeared to be delighted that I had been assigned the role. I was to get thirty pounds a day, which seemed excessive, but all my friends as usual said I should have asked for fifty. The location shots were to be done at Woodstock, outside and around Blenheim Palace. Accommodation had been booked at the Bear Hotel, and thither I repaired. It was still high summer, and one of those rare lovely ones at that. I had read the script, realised that I had the best part in the film, and was sick with terror. However, after meeting Joan Greenwood, with whom I had at least half my scenes,

"I Know the Face, but . . ."

I was greatly reassured. A sweeter, funnier, more disarming lady you could not meet, and I was soon potty about her. Jill Balcon, another charmer, was playing her lady-in-waiting, and the three of us became inseparable.

My dad was played by the late Frederick Valk, who was expecting his first child at the time. He was in consequence fairly restless, and I used to go for long walks with him in the evenings. He was an enormous great dear, who loved England and the English and had indeed bought the *Encyclopaedia Britannica* on the instalment plan, and was working his way quietly through it. One night, for some unknown reason, we were discussing public schools, whose system is or was my pet hate. Freddie asked me where I had been educated.

"Winchester," I replied.

"Vinchester?" he said. "You remember Diana Qvirk?"

"Oh yes, indeed," I replied. "We used to whistle at her in chapel."

He let out a gargantuan laugh.

"I married Diana Qvirk," he said.

I got to know the Valk family very well, and enchanting they were. His sudden death robbed the stage of a fine actor and his children of a most delightful papa. He was very kind to me, and helped me with my German for the captain in *The African Queen*, a role he should actually have played.

Mr Granger had not arrived, and owing to the alarming reports we had heard of his behaviour and language, we were a bit worried. However, Michael Gough, who was surprisingly playing my brother, said he'd just been in a film with Mr Granger, and that he was a dear. It seemed an unlikely description, and we waited anxiously. The "dear" arrived, with the largest car one had ever seen, a caravan dressing-room in tow, and a very smart chauffeur carrying a lot of cases of champagne. These were produced at dinner the same night, and we all had a fairly uncosy meal. Afterwards, the Misses Green-

I Have My Chance (and Miss It)

wood, Balcon and I sat in a little sitting-room discussing the visitor, when he entered, asked for tea for four, and in a few minutes had become a very ordinary and delightful person. We sat up till four, and ended the evening drinking, as far as I can remember, lemon squash and Eno's, a drink to which I'm particularly addicted in hot weather.

Throughout the film he was fantastically kind to me. He must have known my part was a very good one indeed, but he helped me, gave me sound advice and started a friendship that has endured throughout the years. I can see he can make an appalling impression on some people, as he is fiercely intolerant and impatient of inefficiency and phoniness. But to most actors, his behaviour is impeccable, and his generosity to those having a bad time is legendary. It is only when he comes up against two-faced stars, two-headed directors, and inquisitive press gentlemen, that the storm breaks and heaven help anyone within spitting distance. He'll be horrified when he reads this, as I think he secretly likes to be thought an Ogre, about whom years after his demise someone will write something nice.

So there we were at Woodstock, embarking on a film which was to be the crowning achievement of the British cinema. Indeed, a book on the actual shooting of the film was already being planned, and little did they think at this time that they would eventually have to beg Mr Granger to sign a great many copies in order to sell some of the surplus.

My opening scene was unfortunately to be on a horse. I had by this time cleared up the "writing-riding" misunderstanding, and was taking a few lessons from some patient lady equestrian. I came to a sort of understanding with an animal called Peter, but only after some very nasty moments indeed. There was one day when Peter could only be said to be running away with Peter, and I was trying to think how to stop him, when a gentleman in country costume said, "Where do you think you are going, might I ask?" "Oh, I wish I knew," I replied sadly,

"I Know the Face, but . . ."

as I whizzed past him, realising in my flight that it was the Duke of Marlborough in person.

The day came for the first shot. My mistress (in the film), Frau Busche, and I were on our horses, and fortunately it was (they thought) to be a static shot. I say fortunately, because dear Megs Jenkins, who was playing Mrs Busche, dreaded horses, and had made it quite clear, even in her contract, that her horse was not to move. It was really quite a simple scene, although about eight people were required to keep the horses in position, including, now I come to think of it, the director Basil Dearden, who "knew all about horses". But what made me a bit windy was that Peter had been sacked from carrying me, and his successor was a bit haughty, although they assured me that he was more photogenic than Peter, a statement that bored the pants off me. When it came to my turn to throw a purse at a non-existent beggar lady or gent I aimed inaccurately, and hit the snitch of Frau Busche's animal, who was not unnaturally livid and reared up in rage. Miss Jenkins nearly had a fit, and it was several hours before horses, actors and directors made any sense at all.

It wasn't a happy day and I offered my resignation, which I tend to do on the first day of any acting enterprise, because I can always say later on, "Yah boo, I told you so." Basil ignored this, and suggested that I'd better get to know my new horse, and off I slunk into the woods where it refused to move or even say "Neigh".

The next day was worse. We were all posted to a small hill in the grounds of Blenheim. I had everything on, including the kitchen stove, wigs, hats, swords, daggers and a Roussel Belt.

"On the word Action," said Basil Dearden calmly, "I want you to ride as quickly as possible over to that coach where Freddie Valk is standing."

I looked into the far distance where I could see a tiny figure beside a vehicle.

I Have My Chance (and Miss It)

"As quickly as possible?" I asked.

"Yes," said Basil grimly.

"Action" came, and I stuck my foot or heel into the flanks of the horse. It ambled quietly down the slope, and came to a dead stop by some rather nice grass, where it proceeded to have its tea break. We had three like this, and every time the beast stopped at the same place. Basil was in despair.

"We'd better use the riding double," he said coldly.

For some unknown reason I got puce with rage, and demanded another "take".

"Give the horse a great bash," I shouted at its owner, standing by.

Basil yelled "Action", its owner clouted it, and I went off at about a hundred and ten m.p.h. The hat, wig and sword flew off in the first fifty yards, and almost my Roussel Belt, but the horse continued as if possessed, and drew up at its original spot, dead if you know what I mean.

I picked up my wig, my hat, and my sword, and, with as much dignity as I could muster, wandered back. I didn't speak to Basil, but handed him my wig, my hat, my sword and my theoretical notice. I sulked off to a deck-chair to get comforted by Miss Flora Robson. I watched the riding double don my hat, my wig and my sword, and mount the beast. Very professionally he rode off on "Action", and even more professionally the horse stopped at its usual spot. I was beginning to feel very sorry for Freddie Valk, so near and yet so far, and waiting for a horseman who never seemed able to make it. The riding double came back, and Basil, by then almost apoplectic, ordered the owner of the horse into the saddle. He was as thin as a rake, but nonetheless donned my hat, my wig, my sword, but not my Roussel Belt. For the umpteenth time, Basil shouted "Action".

I slumped back in my chair.

"Please, God," I whispered, "let that dear horse stop where it always does."

"I Know the Face, but . . ."

I closed my eyes with this blasphemy, and opened them to see Basil dancing about with fury. My prayers had been answered, and that's why, dear filmgoer, you never saw George-Louis of Hanover ever greet his father in the forest of Celle.

After that, I was kept strictly off a horse, but we went into Oxford to view what are unaccountably called the "the rushes",[1] and the scene where I threw the purse at Frau Horse's busche (I mean Frau Busche's horse) showed us upside down, which is the sort of thing that can only happen to actors like me.

Back at Ealing, everything went smoothly until they asked me to have all my hair cut off. I wasn't v. keen, although they said that it would make my hair grow stronger than ever before, but they experimented with rubber wigs, and finally decided that it would have to be done. Like the great fool that I am, I didn't hold my locks to ransom or I could have paid for some of the treatment I have given my head since that catastrophic day. Mark you, as my mother would say, they did it in the nicest possible way; I did a scene in the morning with all my hair on, and then a Mr Taylor, who has since left for South Africa, shaved my head to within a quarter of an inch or less, and Wham! there was I, plunged into a terrifying sadistic scene with my wife (Miss Greenwood). I now know exactly how the French collaborators felt when they got their deserts, and speaking for myself, I shall never collaborate again. It's torture on the pillow at night, and I finally had to wear one of those little woolly caps which the Arabs wear to show that they have been circumcised, which is that sort of thing anyhow. But I did at least find out who were my true friends. They were the ones who didn't visibly blench when walking with me through the streets. I did really look like something out of a space-fiction book, and the villagers at the place where Mr Granger had his country residence started a

---

[1] Results of the previous day's shooting.

I Have My Chance (and Miss It)

rumour that I was his dotty brother who was kept under lock and key in the attic.

It was singularly unattractive, and I was at low resistance ebb, when I had to start beating the daylights out of my beloved Miss Greenwood. Basil Dearden kept us a great many days on this scene, and it was I who usually ended up crying because blood started trickling out of Miss G's mouth. When you want not to hurt someone, you generally end by doing them mortal injury, and I couldn't bear these scenes, even if the script dictated so. I forgot to explain that I had to be completely bald, in order that the audience would be sufficiently shocked when I took my wig off, before entering the bridal chamber on my wedding night. Shocked they were, and, on the general release, a pretty good giggle was had by north of the river cinema addicts one week, and by south of the river *ditto* the next. Twice I had to be re-shaved before the end of the film, because of an irritating thing called "continuity", and as for "growing stronger", that's the silliest thing I've ever heard. I spent a vast fortune with some ladies in Sloane Street who paint your pate with iodine, which makes you look as if you've been scalped, some sadists in New York, who pour boiling oil on your head, and vibrate it until you are dizzy, to say nothing of sulphur shampoos, magnetic combs, standing on my head, lying at an incline, and other pursuits, in an attempt to bring back my pre-Saraband hair.

But still none of that would have mattered if I'd become a star overnight, and stolen a march on Mr Yul Brynner. The film came out, and I went to the gala-gala première with Mr Granger, and the Press hated it, the public couldn't understand it, and hundreds of thousands of pounds went down the drain. But they adored it in Yugo-Slavia, Japan, and I believe Minorca, and I owe my only steady fan to the film. He is a sex maniac, and lives in Cologne. I say sex maniac, because I cannot imagine an ordinary fan asking for a picture of me wrestling naked.

"I Know the Face, but . . ."

But that is what he did. "I have seen Saraband thrice," he wrote, "and may I say you are delicious in your burliness. To me you are far more handsome than such as Stewart Granger."

Here followed a request for a photo. Funnily enough, I have no pictures handy of me wrestling naked, but my friends, including Mr Granger, on reading this extraordinary letter, insisted on my replying to it, a step which I was to regret.

"Dear Herr W.," I wrote. "Thank you for your nice unusual letter. I'm afraid I have no pictures of me wrestling naked, but perhaps this will do." I enclosed a wartime snap of myself on a camel near the Sphinx, which I regret to say sent my fan delirious with joy.

"My dearest Peter Bull," he wrote. "I cannot tell you what pleasure you with the camel give me. I love you, Peter Bull, and would like to be your big chum. Have you by chance also a picture of your full corporation in bathing drawers?"

This froze me into silence, but he still writes occasionally, and I have a horror that he will suddenly turn up in Chelsea and frighten the daylights out of my daily.

I have had very few fan letters in the course of my career, always excepting the incoherent but enchanting babblings from Ghana. They all read rather like the following:

Dear Sir,

I am very happy to write you this letter. The reason why I write you this letter. I want only of your free photograph, so that I will never forget your name in my life. I have the honour and most respectful to inform you these few lines because I have heard so much of your free photographs and it is very nice for people to see so I beg you to try and send me your nice photographs. I wish to end here this letter.

And "end it here" they usually do, with no legible signature or just "your loving friend" followed by the number of a box, as they all seem to live in Boxes in Ghana.

I Have My Chance (and Miss It)

I answer them all, as I am still trying to get rid of the ones I had printed on postcards, anticipating a vast demand after *Saraband* and showing me in costume, but I can't pretend they come in the category of "nice photographs" and may very easily have contributed to Ghana wishing to become independent.

Basil Dearden was not unnaturally deeply depressed by the public reaction to *Saraband For Dead Lovers*, but he seems to bear me no grudge and even employs me from time to time, although I must admit it is in some role which requires humiliation or violence to be dished out to the character. I am very fond of him indeed and I like it when he rings up as he did the other year and said: "Will you be blown up to-morrow, Peter?" "Yes, of course, Basil," I replied meekly.

So the next day I reported for a film, dressed up to the nines in a Dictator's uniform and was made to kick off at a foreign football match. The whole point of the scene was that the ball, heavily mined, should explode in my face and blow me to smithereens. I do not know if any of you have ever tried running to kick a football and then stopping dead just as your toes connect, but that is what I had to do, so that the shot could be "tricked"; and very difficult it was, I don't mind telling you. It was quite a funny day's work, though I never asked the name of the film, got paid fifty smackers for a morning's work and tootled happily off home.

The next one Mr Dearden engaged me for was even more degrading but a good deal more lucrative. In this film I had to be drenched to the skin, have a pie thrown at my face ("What's the fellow aiming at?" was the cue), have the pie frozen on to my face, chipped off with a chisel by Nick Phipps and end with some icicles hanging on the end of my nose. It wasn't a frightfully attractive part and it was for a comedy called *Who Done It?* I imagine the next offer to come from Mr D. will be one of those lifeboat numbers, where one spends days and nights

"I Know the Face, but..."

getting in and out of the water while the tank, in which the film is being shot, gets smellier and smellier.

I had enough of that in *The African Queen*. Though I was and still am very proud of being in that (to me) superb film, there was one quite horrid day swimming about in a tank which hadn't been emptied for months. I have to admit that Miss Katharine Hepburn was in a boat dishing out the brandy, which made a big difference, but the taste of the water is with me still.

Being chosen to play the German Captain in this film was one of the most exciting things that has happened to me, and I was really desperate to land the job. It all came up very suddenly while I was at the Alexandra Palace, about to embark on the second transmission of a TV play called *The Silent Inn*. It was in this that I enacted the part of the heavyweight champion of the world, although it was written for the lightweight one. We had finished a heavyweight lunch and I was summoned to the phone by my agent just as we were about to embark on a final run-through.

"If you want to play a goodish part in *The African Queen*," he announced, "you have got to be at Isleworth Studios by six."

It was, as you can imagine, not a very convenient appointment, and to get to Isleworth from Muswell Hill is not exactly child's play. You are also forbidden by contract to leave the area when about to transmit, but on the pretence of visiting a not very probable sick friend in hospital at Wood Green, I escaped in a car at about five, without more than a shilling on me, met John Huston, the director of the film, spoke a few words of German for the part, clinched the deal and whirled back to the Ally-Pally, cashed a cheque, paid the chauffeur and went through the TV in a daze.

The trouble, I thought, with the final scenes of *The African Queen* was that the film went to pieces with the arrival of the German Captain, though for once it was not entirely my fault.

I Have My Chance (and Miss It)

After the miraculous long scenes in which Miss Hepburn and Mr Bogart were the sole protagonists, the slightly phoney happy ending was bound to jar. But non-professionally it was a happy time, and I was knocked sideways by the stars' integrity and kindness. On the first day at the studios Miss Hepburn, to whom I had not even been introduced, insisted on the third star dressing-room, which had been empty since Robert Morley's departure, being allotted to me. I had many lunches with her and the Bogart family, and though they teased me a bit about an unfortunate film called *Salute the Toff* in which I was also engaged at the time, I adored being with them.

I did not see the film till some time after it had opened, but I got rather irritated by the number of viewers who asked me if I had used my own voice in the film. It was then that I discovered that indeed my voice had been par-dubbed by Walter Rilla and jolly cleverly at that.

Things were very different in *The Captain's Paradise*, another splendid film. In this I played the chief of a firing-squad deputed to shoot Alec Guinness and whom he eventually had shot by his men after bribing them. I had to speak Spanish throughout, but for some unknown reason they let me get away with it on this occasion. Perhaps it was because my Spanish was so execrable that they thought even the Spaniards would think it was a foreign language, and so no umbrage would be taken in any quarter. The film, it may be remembered, dealt with Captain Alec Guinness having a wife in each port, and was a highly-coloured version of what might happen on the Gibraltar-Tangier ferry. In any case, I gather, the film was banned in Tangier and frowned on in Gibraltar. Tangerines had to go very far afield to find the film.

There had been no location work for the actors, but years later I was in Tangier having a holiday with Sir Alec himself. Not realising what we were doing, we got on the ferry which

"I Know the Face, but..."

was to whisk us off to Gibraltar, and as we boarded the ship a voice behind us said:

"Ah, Mr Guinness, I have wanted to catch up on you for some time. Do you realise that you have made me the laughing stock of the Mediterranean?" Alec, alarmed, turned round and found himself facing the Captain of the ferry-boat. However, he turned out to be a charming, jovial gent who gave us cups of tea on the bridge and helped us to get through the Customs.

Notable films in which I played parts, but never actually appeared on the silver screen, included *The Lavender Hill Mob* and *The Man Who Never Was*. In the former, I played a religious maniac who chased Alec Guinness and Stanley Holloway out of a café in the Tottenham Court Road. It was quite irrelevant to the film, as indeed was my contribution to *The Man Who Never Was*, which resulted in the Part That Never Was as a Spanish Consul at Huelva.

Films in which I have appeared that haven't induced me to go under the seat while watching my contribution can be counted on two hands. They include *Sabotage*, in which Hitchcock gave me my first close-up, and an odd little film called *Young Man's Fancy*, about the Siege of Paris, in which I tried to sell dirty postcards to Griffith Jones and Anna Lee. The film in which I tried to sell dirty postcards to Lilli Palmer (*Sunset in Vienna*) does not come into this category.

In another chapter I shall deal with the unthinkable and unmentionable minor films with which I have been connected, but of the feature films in which I found myself, there are one or two fairly bizarre examples: *As You Like It*, for instance, was a version of Shakespeare's comedy made by Elisabeth Bergner and her director husband Paul Czinner in 1936. It had lovely things in it, but was a quite unsuitable subject for filming. I played William, the yokel, and by that time they had nearly run out of animals for the forest of Arden, and I had to share the scene with a lemur which hung by its tail and was

I Have My Chance (and Miss It)

pretty confused by the man-made trees, and couldn't make up its mind which to choose. This made the scene a bit restless.

Then there was *Night Without Armour* with Miss Dietrich and the late Robert Donat. It is the only film in which I have acted in a complete coma. I was working in *Dreaming Lips* with Miss Bergner at the time, and while wandering around the corridors at Denham Studios, was pounced on and asked if I could come and see Jacques Feyder (Françoise Rosay's husband) who was directing the other big film then on the floor at Denham. He apparently approved of me, and the dialogue director handed me a few lines for a scene to be shot around midnight. It appeared that I was to be a Russian general during the Revolution, but I did not dare to ask whose side I was on. I did however appear in two films on the same day; I left the set of *Dreaming Lips* at 6.30 p.m., bustled off to *Knight Without Armour*, threw a few glasses round the place, screamed at some soldiers, and just after midnight returned to Miss Bergner who was about to throw herself into the Thames, played by the studio floor which was being slowly flooded. I slept in my dressing-room from five to seven, and took a workman's ticket back to London, to which for once I thought I was entitled.

The oddest film in which I got involved was a cinematic mangle of Bridget Boland's interesting play *Cockpit*. This was eventually renamed *The Lost People*, which was a fairly accurate description of the actors recruited for this film, who included Mai Zetterling, Dennis Price, Richard Attenborough, Herbert Lom and Jill Balcon. Also in the cast was a charming International star, an explosive actress who wasn't keen on sharing a dressing-room. The movie was being shot at the tiny Gate Studios at Elstree, where accommodation was strictly limited. The lady was subsequently cut out of the film owing to complete incomprehensibility, which made the cutter's job a little difficult, as she was playing a leading part. However, months after the completion of the film, her scenes were re-

"I Know the Face, but . . ."

shot with another distinguished artiste in the role, but as only one of the original principal players was still available, the re-shooting was restricted. The first lady sued the film company, not because she had been cut out of the film, but because they had left her in by mistake in one long shot and made her (or so she maintained) look like an extra.

My part was a sex maniac called Woolf, a character who did not appear in the play. It was my favourite type of part, as there were only two words to say, which were "Rats, rats". These were fairly easily learnt, and after studying them, I was able to concentrate on the other aspects of the part. Woolf appeared in many scenes, thank goodness, but only making faces in the background. "Woolf sneers", "Woolf looks on furtively", "Woolf leers", "Woolf gives a look of mocking disgust", and so on.

I practised the faces in the Green Line Coach going down to the Studio, which emptied it in no time, and one day I arrived for the wedding of Mai Zetterling and Richard Attenborough. This was to take place on the stage of a disused theatre which was being utilised as the clearing house for displaced persons. I was to stand in the dress circle, and there was to be a long tracking shot, ending up with a gigantic close-up of me, believe it or not. Bernard Knowles, the director, gave me my position, and we had a full rehearsal. I made my face.

"What's that meant to be?" said Bernard, after the rehearsals.

"Mocking disgust," I replied sweetly.

"But it should be anguish," said Bernie.

"Not in my script," I said.

"Well, it was changed yesterday. We have decided to make Woolf sympathetic in this scene."

"Don't think I can do 'anguish'," I complained. "Did 'mocking disgust' all the way up on the bus, and it takes me very long to get motivated."

"Try," he urged.

I Have My Chance (and Miss It)

I did. Made even me feel sick.

Soon after this, I had to rape Miss Zetterling all round the dressing-room. It was very claustrophobic, there was a heat-wave on, and we got giddy racing round. Just as I was about to rape her, she had to stick a dagger in me, and I had to explode a bladder of chocolate sauce to make it look like blood (shades of *Marie Antoinette*). By the end of the day, as I was in a thick seaman's sweater, I ponged appallingly. The day on which I had to say "Rats, rats", I got very excited, and did it. I thought, superbly. I rushed on to report on the plague that was spreading through the theatre, with real tears rolling down my cheeks, and said the two words. Two days later I was asked to post-synchronise them, as they were totally incoherent.

Another unhappy experience was a christening scene in *Woman Hater*, an ill-fated comedy starring Mr Granger and Mme Edwige Feuillère. Irene Handl and I played parents of a child about to be baptised by Miles Malleson. The poor little mite screamed the set down until, oddly enough, lulled into oblivion by Mr Granger.

I will draw an iron curtain over details of a Margaret Lockwood pictures in which I ran round the deck in shorts, a Tom Walls film in which I had to cry during a tennis game, falling out of a stage coach which contained Jean Kent, and pass rapidly on to my perf. as one of the Brothers Grimm in *Contraband*. My contribution was not noteworthy, but I did have a scene in it where I tied up Mrs Profumo (Valerie Hobson to you). This earned me a picture in that splendid paper *London Life*, which dealt with the eccentricities of the human race. At first sight the journal seemed innocuous enough, but on closer inspection was found to be crammed with interesting information. Early pages were devoted to family pictures and details of the Royal Family and Society, but later on one realised that all the photographs were of people with long hair, firmly corseted or in mackintoshes. Even pince-nez came in for close

"I Know the Face, but . . ."

scrutiny and the correspondence columns were full of letters from people who signed themselves under noms-de-plume like lac-Fan", "Mud-Mad", "Madam High-Boot" and the "Maris of the Old Regime", who seemed to be keen on having his staff attired in stiff starch and why not for heaven's sake? Unfortunately somebody lodged a complaint with the Home Secretary during the war and the paper changed its policy, though I was happy to see, in a recent issue, that it was getting back to normal with an article entitled "The Problem of the One-armed Bride".

Oliver Twist was one of the most distinguished films in which I appeared, and though I was not very good in it, David Lean, by miraculous cutting, made me pretty effective, at least so I thought. Then there was or were *Footsteps in the Fog*, with the results of which I was not at all dissatisfied. It was a fairly alarming film into which I was without doubt steered by my friends Mr and Mrs Granger, who were starring in it in Technicolor. I find it doubly windy-making to appear with close friends, and even Sir Alec Guinness, who is kindness itself on the set, sometimes reduces me to a quivering jelly by his own perfection. I always feel that if I am inadequate it will disturb one's personal relationships. So far, touch wood, it hasn't; but I don't find it cosy.

Mr Granger was just finishing his role in *Footsteps in the Fog* when I started mine, and my main job was to be beastly to Mrs Granger in the witness-box. The director was a Mr Arthur Lubin, who usually directs Mules called Francis, and Mr Granger was not potty about him. We started off the day with a "master-shot", which means that the actors go through the entire scene from rather far off and only portions of the shot are likely to be used in the final film. After this Mr Granger did his close-ups in order to save Columbia Pictures the vast fortune they would have had to pay out if they had kept him beyond "the Friday". Mrs Granger and I went back to start our

I Have My Chance (and Miss It)

lunch while he was having his photograph taken. We were giggling away happily when Mr Granger strode in.

"You aren't really going to do it like that, are you?" he asked Mrs Granger and me.

"I thought we were rather good," I said impertinently.

"It's just going to ruin the entire film," replied Mr G.

"Perhaps you'd like to direct me," I said, putting my knife and fork down.

"Of course," he said.

The upshot of all this was that on returning to the set, the director took me aside and said he'd been thinking about the scene during lunch and had decided that I should play it another way. It was, of course, sheer coincidence that his views coincided with those of Mr Granger but, as I have intimated before, Mr Granger has quite a forceful personality.

I had also been squeezed into *Beau Brummel* (starring Mr Granger too) but in this one he had been unable to give me much assistance. I was not frightfully happy playing either Fox or Burke (Mark Dignam played the other) and some wit said we looked more like Burke and Hare.

My two most recent film jobs have both been in Guinness films and as at time of writing I have been unable to check on results, I will wisely hold my peace. I was very happy in both of them and *The Scapegoat* was a wonderful experience, taking me to France for three weeks, a glass factory in Wealdstone for one day and a lunch party in the studios, which lasted nearly a week, in which I had to eat gorgeous *pâté* from Fortnums.

Chapter VI

THE LADY'S NOT FOR BURNING

WHY does one (or perhaps I should say, do I) remember disasters so much more vividly than successes? Certainly, in stage biographies, the Success Story in the theatre is now so hackneyed that the reader must instinctively long for a taste of mishap. To judge from some books of this sort, even if the show has had a short run, it is made abundantly clear that the author or authoress made a great "personal success", whatever that may mean. But let it not be thought that I have never appeared in a success, and I suppose the most distinguished one was *The Lady's Not For Burning*. This production was not only to prove epoch-making in the history of the theatre, but more important still (for me) was to establish a lot of friendships in the company which have lasted to the present day.

It all started when morale, to say nothing of bank balance, was very much in the red, and I had not been allowed to display myself on a stage since the war. A lady I knew, principally as an actress, called Marjorie Stewart, was casting director at the Arts Theatre, at this time administered by Alec Clunes. She sent me a script of the Christopher Fry play, of which I understood about an eighth at first reading, but it was impossible to ignore the beautiful writing and above all the excruciatingly funny jokes dotted through the piece. I was pretty entranced by my part, which only started in the second act but was full of lovely things.

The play was written in verse, but although this fact made the project more intimidating, I could never view it as such, and once I had got used to the language, it seemed no different from ordinary dialogue. The first reading was highly successful,

The Lady's Not For Burning

and we all had the feeling we were embarking on something of exceptional quality. Jack Hawkins was directing, and Alec Clunes was to play the leading male part, Thomas Mendip, a gent who threw a whole village into turmoil by wanting and indeed insisting on being hanged. The part of Jennet Jourdemayne, the girl accused of witchcraft, had been written for Pamela Brown. Owing to her non-availability at this time Sheila Manahan, straight from her great success in *Happy as Larry*, was entrusted with it. The two brothers were played by Michael Gough and Gordon Whiting, the young clerk by Derek Blomfield and his adored one by Daphne Slater. Henzie Raeburn was the Mayor's wife, and the character men were acted by Andrew Leigh (Mayor) Frank Napier (Chaplain) and Morris Sweden, who was to prove wildly funny as the rag-and-bone man, Skipps.

It was only scheduled to run 2½ weeks at the Arts Theatre, as there were previous commitments for the theatre and some of the actors. Financially it was bound to be a wash-out, but somehow the prospect did not worry me. Christopher Fry came to all the rehearsals, and his quiet dry wit and enchanting modesty made the rehearsals gay and relaxed, and the only fly in the ointment was Jack Hawkins breaking his leg during this period and having to direct in agony and plaster.

The play went very well on the first night, March 10th, 1948, but the notices were mixed. Some critics opined that the meaning was obscure and difficult to follow, but most of them had the good sense to realise that it was a new type of verse play. There was, however, no doubt about its popular appeal to the patrons of the arts or indeed the Arts, and we were packed for the short run. One's actor friends raved about it, and Miss Hermione Gingold came both Sundays. The dressing-rooms on the Sunday nights were thronged with stars, and it was quite droll one night, when the rafters had rung with praise and all the usual vociferous utterances of fellow actors saying

"I Know the Face, but . . ."

"darlings, darlings, it was wonderful, marvellous, divine," when an old school friend of mine tapped at the door and said, "Thought I'd come and see you to tell you that I've had a most interesting evening and this is John Abercrombie who didn't like it at all," and a rather sad bespectacled gent was ushered into the room to face a lot of rather hysterical artistes.

We were all desperately sad when the run finished, and I suppose the general feeling was that *The Lady's Not For Burning* would not be heard of again. For no one seemed anxious to buy the play for the commercial theatre, and had it not been for an energetic lady called Daphne Rye, it probably would never have had a slap-up London production. Miss Rye was at that time casting director for H. M. Tennent Ltd., and came to the last performances at the Arts. Indeed on tickets supplied, but not I think paid for, by me. She was lyrical in her praise for the entire evening, and hastened off to Mr "Binkie" Beaumont, the astute head of the firm, to persuade him to buy it lock, stock and barrel for the West End.

"What's it about, Daphne dear?" he is reported to have asked.

"Well," said Daphne, "it's about a witch who isn't a witch who falls in love with a man who wants to be hanged."

"Ye-e-e-e-s," said Binkie, "And then what, dear?"

"They spend the night in the gaol, and are let off the next morning."

"It doesn't sound very dramatic," said Binkie. "Is there a surprise twist at the end?"

"Oh yes, there's an old rag-and-bone man called Skipps who has nothing to do with anything and comes on trailing a lot of cans, dead drunk, and it's all marvellous and ends happily."

When further pressed about the plot, she is said to have burst into tears, because she couldn't explain why she had loved it. So that was that. But nothing daunted, Miss Rye got hold of a script and sent it to John Gielgud, who was just back

The Lady's Not For Burning

from a long season in America and was about to have one of his rare failures with a revival of *The Return of The Prodigal*. He was enchanted by the Fry play, and decided (I believe, against every advice) to play the leading part and co-direct it with Esmé Percy. Having embarked on the production, he rather wanted to make a clean sweep, but Christopher Fry insisted on Frank Napier and, luckily, me being retained. The tragedy was that Frank died before the production, and was robbed of what I am certain would have been a notable success, ensuring him a lasting niche in the theatre. For me, there will never be another Chaplain, though the late Eliot Makeham, who eventually played it, was very good indeed. But Frank, who was desperately ill when he played it at the Arts, gave it an unearthly quality which was unique. When he said the line "I am not really here, you know," it brought the house down, but it was a laugh made more poignant to us by the fact that he almost wasn't there himself. He was in great pain, and I can still see him sitting like a great big black bat at the side of the stage at the Arts, all through the interval, because he couldn't face the stairs up to his dressing-room.

I was frankly terrified of working with John Gielgud, and it was quite clear that in those days he was pretty bored by frightened actors. But it was my first major part in the West End and my morale, not helped by not acting at the Memorial Theatre, Stratford-on-Avon, was not very high. Oh, those rehearsals! Sir John has a quicksilver brain, and chops and changes so many things in one rehearsal that you have no time to write it down until afterwards, and soon your script looks like a patchwork quilt. Most of the company were reduced to tears at some period, and one member succumbed to jaundice and disappeared into the night. Anything I had done at the Arts was ruthlessly exorcised, and I had to fall back on my lines which, it must be admitted, were very fine indeed. I also was helped enormously by having a dear friend in the cast, namely,

"I Know the Face, but . . ."

Miss Pamela Brown, who was now playing the *soi-disant* witch.

Miss B. had been in my Perranporth company for two seasons and had added great lustre thereto. She was now technically a "star" owing to her zonking success as Claudia, a character I am sure she despised to the roots of her being. Jennet Jourdemayne was a different cup of tea and she played it most beautifully. During the war Christopher Fry had produced her in many plays at the Oxford Playhouse, and as she had worked with Gielgud, frequently to their mutual benefit, this part of the production went pretty smoothly. Pam is the opposite of most leading ladies, in that she rarely speaks unless she has something worth saying and can on occasions be very witty indeed. She was once rung by a famous management, who asked:

"Pamela, could you do Hedda Gabler very quickly at the Lyric, Hammersmith?"

There was a short pause.

"Do you mean SPEAK it very quickly?" asked Miss Brown.

Among her favourite roles, she confesses, are long parts in films which require the minimum of speaking but which lurk in the background on a daily rate and look enigmatic for weeks on end. Her contributions to *The Tales of Hoffman* and *Richard III* thus suited her admirably. It is reported that Sir Laurence Olivier rang her up rather tentatively about the latter. The role he had in mind was Lady Jane Shore, a key part in the production, but he had his doubts about her accepting it owing to the paucity of dialogue.

"You see, Pam, the trouble is that there aren't any lines," he said.

"No LINES?" shouted Miss Brown down the blower.

"No, I'm afraid not," said Sir Laurence, abashed.

"Snap," said Miss Brown quietly.

However, in *The Lady's Not For Burning* she was to speak a great many lines for months on end. She was to make an enormous impression both in London and New York, and few

The Lady's Not For Burning

people who witnessed the piece will forget her first entrance past the window, with red hair flying, and her sinking exhausted on to the floor after being pursued through the town by the angry populace. The action of the play took place "around the fourteenth century", and for some reason Oliver Messel's most beautiful set unfortunately had no proper exit through the centre door. Owing to the realistic perspective of the backcloth, those involved in the second act could not creep off to their dressing-rooms and therefore had to pretend that they were going off into the adjoining room and in fact do just that. The only difficulty was that the room they went into was in reality a cubby-hole in which Harcourt Williams (the Mayor), Eliot Makeham (Chaplain), Richard Leech (who played the lecherous brother, Humphrey), and I had to sit for all of twenty minutes while Miss Brown and Sir John played a very long love scene. For the first few weeks I listened to it sometimes (and this is not affectation), being so moved that I used to wet my peepers, but later on we fell back on our own devices through boredom. And it was quite a surprise to the audience when one night the door flew open to disclose the Messrs Leech and Bull deep in an acrimonious game of chess, Eliot Makeham reading a rather lurid thriller, and Harcourt Williams plainly doing the *Daily Telegraph* Crossword. The young lovers were played by Richard Burton and Claire Bloom, and it is certain that this production set them both on the road to fame. Richard clearly had an exceptional talent. His sincerity and physical beauty were deeply impressive, and when he scrubbed the floor during the long love scene before mentioned, it was obvious that a new star was in embryo, even on his knees.

The remainder of the Mayor's family were played by Nora Nicholson, who brought wit and acerbity to the wife, and David Evans (Nicholas), who had a corncrake voice which issued out of a small compact body with droll results. I shared

"I Know the Face, but . . ."

a dressing-room with him for over a year and we never exchanged a cross word which is, I believe, a European record. Esmé Percy played the rag-and-bone man, Skipps, and he was a bit worrying to act with, as he had a knack of never giving remotely the same performance. He had a unique personality and was a very lovable man of great sweetness and a marvellous raconteur. I can only hope that he has regaled the angels in heaven with the tale of the Tuesday matinée at Leeds when his glass eye fell out through his exuberance. We were all conscious of his affliction, and in moments of supreme bad taste had made suggestions of what we would do if an accident occurred. These varied from breaking into a song and dance to the tune "You've got your Eye On Me", to turning the play into one about Nelson quite suddenly.

But when it actually happened, we were all thunderstruck and quite incapable of even going on with the play. There was Esmé hopping about, looking for the damned thing which had slid down my capacious robe and fallen tinkling to the ground. It was simply no help Esmé whispering to the world in general, "Don't tread on it. It cost eight guineas." If it had cost 8,000 guineas, I doubt if I could have uprooted myself from my particular spot. Finally, Richard Leech found it and returned it to the owner, but after all, as we said to each other afterwards in Fullers (black coffee with the Buck Rarebits after that ordeal), he (Richard) was still a fully qualified doctor. The trouble was that it was the first of many similar incidents, and Oliver Messel had designed a beautiful patch for Esmé, who looked like a dear rather artistic pirate in it.

But I am anticipating more than somewhat and the Leeds incident occurred quite late in the pre-London tour, which was interminable and at some points downright disheartening. The provincial audiences seemed not to be able to make head or tail of the play. Only in Newcastle and Birmingham did we find real warmth and appreciation and a faint hope that disaster

The Lady's Not For Burning

did not lie in wait for us in London, and many's the time the management and Sir John must have felt like calling the whole thing off. We reached the nadir of depression at Northampton where we played Holy Week to a stony silence. Apart from a visit to the Boot Museum (v. sinister), it was not a happy time and the New Theatre's policy did not help our morale. For, due to follow us as an attraction, was a Variety Show featuring "Real Frogmen in a Real Tank" and the front of the theatre was plastered with pictures of the daring gentlemen. So obscured were the details of our piece that one patron left the theatre in a rage shouting, "If they advertise frogmen I want to see frogmen" and didn't even wait till the last act to see if one popped up. We did suggest to Esmé that he might play Skipps as a rag-and-frogman, but he declined.

All through the tour we rehearsed incessantly and the company did get to know and love one another, but I think everyone was astounded at the warmth of the reception when we finally opened at the Globe Theatre, on May 11th, 1949. It was evident from the moment the curtain went up that for once a first-night audience had come to enjoy themselves and with a unanimous Press we were in for a very long run. It was also an absurdly happy one, and David Evans and I settled down cosily in our dressing-room on the second floor. We had a fine view of the disorderly house across the way and kept a lot of impertinent charts on our wall. One was a graph of Esmé Percy's performance, and there was a sheet, written entirely in code, tabulating marks given to Visitors in the Dressing-Room. The poor unsuspecting victim was under close scrutiny, and after his or her exit was judged on Sincerity, Intelligence, Charm, Grace and Beauty of Movement, and of course Liking Us, etc., etc. After a short time we became very daring indeed and the Unvisited used to mark the Guest of the Visited while He, She or They were still in the room, thereby plunging the other occupant of dressing-room 7 into a tee-hee of nerves and appre-

"I Know the Face, but . . ."

hension and quite often hysterics. Unfortunately a lot of people got to hear about it, and towards the end of the run one noticed people carrying out some very curious evolutions. Indeed, Paul Scofield came in after a matinée and, having executed some elaborate Grace and Beauty of M., said that he'd loved it all and he knew we wouldn't believe him but it was his opinion that ours were the outstanding performances in the play. This gave Mr Scofield 10 out of 10 for practically everything, and made him equal with Miss Jean Simmons, hitherto our top scorer.

During the long run we were never allowed to get stale, mainly because Sir John Gielgud is a perfectionist and keeps on altering a production which he has directed. If he is appearing in the play as well, one has no chance of slacking, as his eyes are all over the place, and many's the time he would change an entire scene between a matinée and evening performance.

"I think you're getting a bit stale, Peter," he would remark of a Saturday just before the evening performance. "Try playing the last scene from the opposite side of the stage."

I would remonstrate half-heartedly, knowing he was right, take a nip of brandy before going on for the scene and make a hash of it.

"Sorry. Go back to the old way" would say Sir John after the perf. But he had scored his point and one became more alert. There was a pretty extraordinary evening when he wanted all those hidden behind the door in the second act to burst out with more excitement and dash, making up exclamations as they ran. Even the old hands, the Messrs Williams and Makeham, boggled a bit at this.

"Couldn't we rehearse it once?" they asked.

"No," said Sir John, "it will spoil the excitement."

So that evening out we came with more excitement and dash than you would believe possible. But unfortunately a series of mishaps were to befall which negatived the effect. Both Harcourt Williams and Eliot Makeham, by some strange coinci-

The Lady's Not For Burning

dence, let out an identical exclamation, which plunged them into hysterics. I collided with Richard Leech, who knocked into Pamela Brown, who collapsed on the floor. As it was only a few minutes before she was meant to faint dead away, this was not going to help the plot. Suddenly I caught sight of Richard Burton who had stopped scrubbing the floor to stare at us with glazed horror. As he had had no warning of the change, he thought we had taken leave of our senses.

"Sorry, chaps," muttered Sir John, "entirely my fault," as the curtain fell and we all dissolved into more helpless laughter. No wonder we were all potty about him, and as far as I am concerned he personifies the theatre at its highest and most noble. His enthusiasm and energy are boundless, and though he can be a hard taskmaster, most of the results are worth it. He has a notoriously quick tongue which has caused him to drop enough "bricks" to build a National Theatre.

A typical one was when we made a recording of the play during the New York run. The following evening I popped into his dressing-room.

"Oh, Peter, you were quite good in the recording," said my hero, but the emphasis was so much on the last word that it gave me a saddening clue as to what he had thought of my stage performance for the past eighteen months.

During the run I had the honour to be asked by him to be in a scene from *Richard of Bordeaux*, in which he was to play his original part for a special charity "do" at the Coliseum.

"Would you play the Archbishop of York, Peter?" he asked, and as an afterthought said, "You see, you can wear your *Lady's Not For Burning* costume," which took a little of the gilt off the gingerbread, I must admit.

Sir John was going to do the last scene of the play and Richard Burton was to play the faithful Maudelyn. Richard Leech, Harcourt Williams and I supported them. *Richard of Bordeaux* had been Sir John's first great success in the commercial theatre

"I Know the Face, but . . ."

at the New Theatre in 1933. We rehearsed in the Globe and I shan't easily forget the first time we read it. Sir John sat in a chair wearing a hat and reading from a script. Suddenly he threw hat and script away and played the rest of the scene word-perfect with tears rolling down his cheeks. We were moved to speechlessness and very near tears ourselves. In fact, the whole thing was a bit weepy, even though David said, with a certain amount of cause, that I looked like a cross between Superman and Blériot flying the Channel. I think this simile was due to a rather unsuitable hat. But the performance provided plenty of thrills, and it's the only time I've been on a stage while a fellow-artist brought the house down. And that's what Sir John did. After the scene we made our way through all the chorus ladies of London, who were waiting to go on and beat the hell out of *There's No Business Like Show Business*, and they parted like the Red Sea to let Sir John through. With glistening eyes he turned to us and said, "Thanks, chaps; well, we had a jolly good blub anyhow."

At the beginning of 1949 the last weeks of *The Lady's Not For Burning* were announced in spite of the continued good business, but Sir John was due at Stratford-on-Avon. There were rumours of an American production, but it obviously would not take place till the autumn.

I filled in the gap with TVs, an occasional film and a bizarre production of *Pericles* about which you will hear later, and in September we started rehearsing for *The Lady* again. There were two changes in the cast: George Howe took over from Harcourt Williams, and a talented young actress called Penelope Munday played Alison. Claire Bloom was released to play in *Ring Round the Moon*, another's bull's-eye for Christopher Fry who adapted it. And while we are on the subject, there was a very memorable production by Sir John of Fry's *Boy With a Cart* at the Lyric, Hammersmith, in which Richard Burton and the late Mary Jerrold gave touching and beautiful performances. Richard indeed was for Frying that year (1950), as he also played the soldier in *A Phoenix Too Frequent.*

Except for him and his wife Sybil and the Richard Leeches, who all went by boat, the rest of the company flew *en masse,* and it was not a very attractive mode of arriving in America this time. We embarked on the plane one night after saying farewell to friends and relatives, and were bundled out again and sent home. Not very convenient for those like Penny Munday and me who had let their flats, but kind Miss Pamela Brown took us home to hers, where we spent an uneasy night wondering if we would ever make Boston in time to open. We got off in fact early the next morning, but it wasn't the end of our tribulations. We touched down at the desolate Gander airport, and for several hours there seemed no chance of our leaving that day. As we didn't have a single cent between us owing to the currency regulations, we could not even buy a Coca-Cola, though Esmé Percy did offer to go round the airport lounge, doing his impressions of Sarah Bernhardt in order to raise some capital.

We finally left, and arrived very early indeed in the morning at New York. The Customs officials seemed almost as sleepy as we were. However, I was asked to open my suitcase which I did. The official picked on a small box which contained a lot of tiny figures which Miss P. Brown gave me. They are really part of a railway set and I take them whenever I go anywhere abroad as they like a change, and if they get tired, there are always the seats marked "Waterloo" or "Aylesbury" on which they sit. I have never bought the train to go with them, though I have riveters, guards, trunks, porters and even lavatories in my collection. The Customs gentleman opened the box gingerly.

"What are these?" he asked.

"People," I replied blandly.

"Why are there holes in the box?"

"*I Know the Face, but . . .*"

"So that they can breathe."

That reply made his examination of my luggage pretty cursory, as I had patently frightened the daylights out of him. He turned to Miss Pamela Brown (we were the only Bs) and asked her kindly to explain the dead flowers that she had in her luggage.

"I like them," said Miss Brown quietly, and the man departed quickly to the easier task of examining Esmé Percy's jewel case.

We were driven into New York, and arrived before dawn, where the Burtons had waited up and we went on a magical tour of the city before retiring to bed. We only had a night in New York before leaving for Boston, and we had a dress-rehearsal on the Monday afternoon preceding the *première*. Mr and Mrs Alfred Lunt, who were appearing simultaneously in Boston, attended it and were encouraging and flattering. The first night went smoothly and the reviews were wholly favourable. I had a wonderful time in Boston, thanks to kind friends' introductions, and I will spare you the usual boring clichés about how much more like England Boston is than England, etc. I was taken to all the places of historical and pictorial interest and it seemed fresh and new and enchanting.

The opening in New York at the Royale Theatre on November 8th, 1950, was a curious experience, because whereas they had laughed generously at the play in Boston and been obviously intrigued by it, the New Yorkers at the three public pre-views sat as quiet as mice and never made a movement. We were depressed and thought we were in for a disaster, and the actual first-night crowd were not much better except for dear faithful Hermione Gingold, who laughed loud and long at all HER favourite jokes, which didn't seem to coincide with those of the rest of the audience. We took several curtain calls, but it wasn't till the rave notices in the papers next morning that we realised we were a hit. In New York you must have favourable reviews in the two main papers, the *Times* and the *Herald*

The Lady's Not For Burning

Tribune or you might as well close the building, even if ALL the other papers are mad about you. Also, there is no such thing in the theatre there as "word of mouth", and many's the play with a great deal of appeal for the general public which has vanished overnight in a welter of critical disdain.

The net result of the notices was fascinating. The second performance was strangely enough a matinée and a riot at that. Old ladies fell tumbling into the aisles, and it was obvious that now they knew it was a comedy, they could be permitted to enjoy themselves. I settled down happily in a strange hotel called the Henry Hudson, which had a swimming-pool, three restaurants and an anglophile director called John Paul Stack who had a mania for old English cars. I had a tiny room on the twenty-first floor with a balcony which gave me a magical view of New York. There were plenty of shows to see and every Sunday night there was a benefit performance of one of the successes for charity, which was a splendid idea. Pam Brown and I managed to get enough seats for *Guys and Dolls* to give them as Christmas presents to the company. One of my biggest thrills was meeting many of the *New Yorker* contributors in the apartment of my idol, Charles Addams. A striking feature of his home was a glass case of the type in which most people keep their china, but his case was dedicated to model guillotines, gallowses and lethal weapons.

A good many droll things happened both on and off the stage. For instance, there was the night when Miss Brown said that her father was "Lost in the soup" instead of "Lost in a search", which only registered on her and Sir John several seconds later. Then there was the night of the biggest laugh of the run. It occurred after the curtain had been up on the third act for a few minutes, and the audience noisily dissolved into hysterics. As no one had said anything remotely funny, the Messrs Gielgud, Evans and Leech had a quick look at their costumes to see if anything had split and tried to get on with the

"I Know the Face, but . . ."

scene. It was not until they had got into the wings that they were told that the coloured commissionaire, who usually stood outside the Royale Theatre, had wandered backstage to give a message, had lost his way, and popped his dark becapped head through Mayor Tyson's window. It is possible that the audience thought that it was another inspired quirk of Christopher Fry's, but unfortunately he couldn't be bribed to do it again.

Then there was the laughable incident of Miss Brown's photograph. One night after the show some of us had visited an amusement arcade and gone into one of those booths where you have your photograph taken and developed while you wait. Miss Brown had bought an enchanting hat, and I suggested that she should have some pictures taken of her in it. I took her the next night to the same booth and was rather bossy with my experience of the machine. I told her not to move while the light was on and in what direction to look. I put the 25 cents into the machine, and Miss Brown sat there still and radiant in her new hat. When the light went out I told her she could relax, and stood by waiting for the finished result. The photograph came through into the slot after a minute and I took one look and handed it to her.

"Think you must have moved," I commented. On the photograph was a lady with a bare behind in Russian boots. We laughed till the tears rolled down our cheeks and up to this very date no satisfactory explanation can be found. Whether some manufacturer of pornography had been caught in the act and had to leave before the results of his or her labour, or whether it had been placed there as a joke, I shall never know; but it became the Great Photo Mystery for the cast of *The Lady's Not For Burning* for many a long day.

Backstage at the Royale was fairly sordid. I was amazed at the squalor of the dressing-rooms, and even our oldest theatres compare favourably with those in New York. Under the tables there was vintage chewing-gum, the doorkeeper was impersonal and never there, and the approach to the stage door became inches under water when the weather was inclement. We shared the passage with two other companies, one of which was *South Pacific*, and it was quite a usual sight to see the exquisite Mary Martin wade through into her theatre. She paid us the compliment of slipping across several times during her waits and watching bits of our play from the wings.

During the run we were all engaged for a radio version of *Hamlet* for the Theatre Guild of the Air. Sir John kindly worked us all into it, and it was a strange experience, as I had never realised the incredible carry-on connected with these productions. There was a last public run-through in a packed theatre, there were introductions of all the artistes, who had to bow to the audience, and a ruthless cutting of the play down to an hour and a quarter in order to enable someone to bang on about United States Steel. Since then, of course, I have worked for commercial TV, but somehow one does not get personally involved in the commercial aspect. Sir John sailed through it all calmly and with such dignity that we were all immensely proud of him.

At the end of the New York run we played a fortnight in both Washington and Philadelphia. In the former we played at a very old-fashioned theatre indeed called the National, with a restricted depth to the stage. I have put this bit of information in because Sir John told the Messrs Howe, Makeham, Leech and myself that he was very sorry, but just for this week we would have to stay on the stage behind the door during the second act love scene. We did not have the heart to tell him that we had been doing this for the last eighteen months anyhow.

In Philadelphia some of us stayed in a remarkably unconventional hotel which reached a new high in sordidity, but we were only charged fifteen dollars a week. To our delight some of the Burlesque Theatre ladies were staying there too. They clocked in on the Sunday night and were doing strip-

"I Know the Face, but . . ."

teases at 0001 hours on Monday morning, to conform with the laws of the city. They were hard-working girls and their show was of course delightfully old-fashioned. In another theatre in this city we saw a musical called *A Tree Grows in Brooklyn* with an unforgettable performance by Shirley Booth, which shone like an opal, warm, glittering and true.

Regretfully we all parted company in New York at the end of April and went our several ways. I took off for California for an extraordinary three months, which now seems like a bad dream. I went to stay with the Grangers and nearly landed parts in both *Rommel* and *Androcles and the Lion*. However, I did not in fact work at all, and indeed spent most of my savings. I cannot regard it as a complete waste of time owing to what I learned about life in Hollywood (second instalment); I think all this knowledge is stored away safely somewhere, but I can only remember ridiculous things about this visit.

I recall vividly trying with Mr Granger to save the lives of his goldfish, who were suffocating from the mud (symbolic, as I said to Mr G.). Then there was Gabriel Pascal's swimming-pool, which was exactly like the one Miss Swanson possessed in *Sunset Boulevard*, though there were leaves at the bottom of Pascal's instead of persons. Other things to remember were the looks on everyone's faces when Jean Simmons announced at a smartish party that she'd been playing tennis on the Santa Monica Public Courts for free, Peter Glenville's yells when he thought he'd been attacked by a tarantula in Gladys Cooper's house, and Marlene Dietrich destroying my illusions in one night by eating vast quantities of hamburgers and sauerkraut in *Hamburger Heaven*. To counteract all this there was the hospitality and kindness dispensed by George Cukor and others and above all the unchanging face and nature of Miss Jean Simmons.

Apart from this, Hollywood seemed a morass of unhappy and insecure people with a layer of masks over their faces and souls which were not worth uncovering—and anyhow you can read all this sort of stuff in any of the novels about the celluloid city. I came home with very little money and three stone lighter in weight. This had been achieved by stringent dieting and ghastly exercises, in order that I might amaze my friends and relations who had been convinced that I would come back swollen considerably. It also enabled me to tackle my first job on my return, which was surprisingly to play the heavyweight wrestling champion of the world on TV.

Chapter VII

SUCCESS STRIKES AGAIN

I DID not have to wait long for another play on my return from the States. It was to prove another very happy engagement and to provide me with what, up to date, is my favourite part. The piece was *Figure of Fun*, a comedy by Arthur Macrae adapted from André Roussin's *Bobosse*. Like *Goodness, How Sad!* it was a play about theatrical people, but it dealt with the difference between fact and fiction. The first act was entirely devoted to a scene from a play within the play, and it was immensely difficult to convey the subtlety to an English audience. In Paris they just popped a prompt box downstage centre; but the average London audience would have thought that this represented a contemporary fireplace or something. In an attempt to solve the problem we all played the act at immense speed; but a lot of people had no inkling of what we were getting at, and the critics thought it the weakness of the play.

My character was a M. Jacques Lambert, a radio reporter who stuttered. It was much a hit-or-miss part and caused me great waves of despair as I rehearsed. He only appeared in the first and third acts, but it was a supporting actor's dream. He opened the play with the leading actor (John Mills), who played the leading actor (Freddie)—if you follow me—who was standing on his head at the beginning of the play within a play. You do see how tricky it all was. The stutterer comes in and can hardly get a word out, which bewilders Freddie, who is expecting to be interviewed by him in a few minutes on the air. The reporter has brought all his equipment with him and in a short time has set it up. Suddenly he stutters that they are on the air and immediately his power of speech becomes crystal clear

Success Strikes Again

and he goes like a bat out of hell in a long spiel which reduces Freddie to near silence. It is he now who can hardly get a word out, or indeed in, and at the end of the broadcast the reporter relapses into incoherence again immediately they are off the air, and exits (except at matinées) to a pretty good round of applause.

The actor playing Jacques could then retire to his dressing-room for well over an hour before descending for the extremely funny third act which begins again by being a "play within a play". This time Freddie the actor is tight and never on the stage when he should be, and the other actors have to cover up and prompt him from behind sofas and things. John Mills was excruciatingly funny in this part of the play, and there was a marvellously contrived surprise twist at the end, which afforded him the opportunity of being moving and true. But in the drunk bits he could go as far as he liked, and many's the time he wound my microphone cable round my crutch so that I couldn't move, much less make an exit. I got the giggles pretty consistently, I'm afraid, towards the end of the run, but I've never enjoyed a part so much and looked forward every evening to a scene with Arthur Macrae (wonderfully expert as the actor's chum). In this we were left waiting on the stage for Freddie to appear. It was a miracle of comic invention and we just stood helplessly inventing dialogue of the type:

"Where can Freddie be?"

"Oh, he can't be long now."

"I think I hear him."

But of course it was hours before Freddie, or rather John Mills, came bounding in, as often as not from some totally unexpected corner of the stage. After that it was bedlam and I thought wildly funny from every possible point of view. It was unfortunately the sort of play that seems frightfully witty even to the actors, which is always dangerous to somebody like me, who, when freed from terror, relaxes too much; and it

"I Know the Face, but . . ."

wasn't much help to my self-control to come on one night and find I had to play one scene facing an enormous photograph of myself dressed in my *Lady's Not For Burning* costume.

We started rehearsing in September 1951 and opened in Manchester on October 1st. It was not a very satisfactory start to the play and it was obvious that a lot would have to be changed. The monologue for Freddie was cut by John Mills, as it simply didn't translate into English. It's funny that in England there is no satisfactory word to compare with "cocu" in the French. Use "cuckold" and the audience immediately think they are at a Restoration Comedy, or the old ladies think it's a town in Sussex. So that scene had to go, as it dealt exclusively with the subject. At the end of the week, which had been fraught with drama both on and off the stage, a miracle happened. Peter Brook, who had wandered up to see his future bride Natasha Parry, who played John Mills' wife, was persuaded to "work" on improving the production. In one short week-end he had re-produced the first two acts, given the cast their morale back, with the result that we opened the first night in Leeds with what was virtually a new show. It went a great deal better there and, though we were tired and a bit shaky by the end of the week, it looked as if disaster had been averted.

We opened at the Aldwych Theatre the following week to a splendid audience who cheered themselves hoarse, a pretty unanimous press and the certainty of a fair run. It was an enchanting cast and there were several rather more than usually bewitching ladies, namely Brenda Bruce, Joyce Heron, Lana Morris and of course the lovely Miss Parry. It was to be one of those rare occasions when one could not wait to get down to the theatre and hob-nob with the chums, and parties were frequent and delightful. I had an enormous dressing-room in which I could do my stomach exercises and I longed for the play to go on for ever. It was not to be, and around March 1952, after I had been in it for six months, I was asked to take over a

Success Strikes Again

part in *Under the Sycamore Tree*, which was on tour with Alec Guinness and Diana Churchill and due in London at any moment. It was by a coincidence destined for the Aldwych Theatre, but I was, in theory, to join the company at Golders Green and Streatham before it actually opened in the West End.

The last four weeks of *Figure of Fun* were announced, but there were several snags to my leaving the cast. The principal one was to find a replacement who would satisfy Mr Mills and others concerned in the production, though my new offer came from the same management (H. M. Tennent Ltd.). It is always infuriating to the rest of the cast, particularly at the end of a run, to have to rehearse because someone has got another job. I was incredibly lucky in that I persuaded Nicholas Phipps, who suddenly had a little time on his hands, to take over. He was surprisingly able to take over also my beret, shirt, shoes, but brought his own moustache to the role.

My last night in *Figure of Fun* (a Friday night, to enable Nick to have a double run on the Saturday) was very sombre for me, and instead of Johnny Mills doing a lot of unthinkable things on the stage to me, it all went depressingly smoothly and I hated the thought of having to say my last line as I exit-ed over the cut-out bit of scenery which represented the roofs of Paris:

"In that case I shall go and take my make-up off."

The next day I went down to Brighton to have a thorough look at what I was letting myself in for on the following Monday. It was difficult to believe that I was actually going to play the General at Golders Green in *Under the Sycamore Tree* in less than 50 hours, though I had rehearsed fairly fully. It was a strange play and not entirely conventional in that all the characters were ants. The company were friendly and a great comfort, and it was a relief to know that the gentleman I was replacing had asked for his release himself. There was therefore no question of guilt or unpleasantness, which so often arises on these occasions. Oliver Messel had designed me a

"I Know the Face, but . . ."

magnificent costume for the occasion, which consisted of an orange pair of riding-breeches, an orange shirt, and a splendid helmet which had a curtain attached to it, so that I could pull a string and show my face when speaking. On the first night at Golders Green I would have liked to have had the curtain permanently drawn. On my feet I had enormous riding-boots which meant a rather studied entrance down the ramp of the ants, or otherwise I slid down on by bottom.

Alec Guinness played the Prime Minister Ant who marries the Queen (Diana Churchill), and Ernest Thesiger (attached to vast antennae) played her adviser. The young ants, on whom experiments in human love were conducted, were played brilliantly by Daphne Anderson and Eric Porter, and Peter Glenville had directed it superbly, so that everything possible was wrung out of this strange play by Sam and Bella Spewak. Most of the play was a great lark, with underlying satire, but what made it so special was Alec Guinness's remarkable and moving transformation in the last act, when he became a very old ant indeed. He did this entirely by genius, as he had only a short interval in which to achieve it. I used to watch him make minor alterations to his face and suddenly become ancient and real.

I had nothing much to do or say in the play except shout myself into a frenzy (which I did with great ease), try not to get the giggles (more difficult), and rush up and down stairs so that Mr Thesiger's wonderful chauffeur-valet, Mr Cox, could ease me in and out of those ghastly boots. Ernest kept us enthralled with stories of High Society, and Alec and I got a great craze for doing the pools, which slightly disrupted the Saturday performances. No wins were registered, however, throughout the run by either party. I went through Golders Green in a daze and the next week we went to Streatham Hill. The following week, on April 23rd, 1952, we opened at the Aldwych to an enthusiastic audience who laughed their heads off. The Press were favourable, though most of the critics complained that it

Success Strikes Again

was a waste of Mr Guinness's immense talent, which was just plain silly of them, as he gave such enormous pleasure to the viewer. I settled down in my old dressing-room, and the play continued till the late autumn when, in spite of continued good business, *Under the Sycamore Tree* was withdrawn to let Alec carry out a film assignment to which he was committed. He was in fact irreplaceable, and though an American production has frequently been mooted, nothing has ever come of it.

This was the first of a series of roles for which I was not in fact the first choice. I never mind taking over a part, as it usually means that they will put up with rather more inadequacies than usual. In January 1954, I was sent for hurriedly by Peter Brook, to read a part in the newest Christopher Fry play *The Dark is Light Enough*. It was that of Dame Edith Evans's medical adviser, and it meant that she had to address me as "Little Doctor" throughout, ("Largeish Doctor" did not quite fit in with Mr Fry's verse). I was therefore battling against heavy odds, but it was nice to be in another of my favourite author's plays and be directed by P. Brook again. Otherwise it was not a very gay time and we had an endless and depressing tour with numerous rehearsals. The only thing that got me through this tour was the constant wit and good humour of John Moffatt, whose eating capacity rivalled mine, and we were to be the constant bane of landladies who unwisely asked us (but only once) if we had had enough. I shudder to think how many buck rarebits and roes on toast went whizzing down our tiny gullets, but I do remember we got enough at Mrs Bishop's in Birmingham. She was a Bishopette really, because she was tiny, and thought us the most eccentric clients she'd ever had. We used to come in after the show, laden down with pickles, chutneys and sauces, and every evening she would place a pound of cheese under the huge cover, and every night she would come in later and find a mouse's portion left, which sent her off in hysterics and to the arms of Mr Bishop.

"I Know the Face, but . . ."

Other diversions were going on long drives with Christopher Fry, with whom I visited Beatrix Potter's house in the Lake District, and trying to find all the old postcards that we could lay our hands on. In junk shops nowadays it is quite possible to find a whole collection of cards from some auction sale which *in toto* give a clear impression of life in the early nineteen-hundreds. These you either send to your friends with the original message on, or cross out the words that no longer apply, like hansom-cabs or horse-buses.

We opened at the Aldwych on April 30th, 1954, and ran through the year. It lasted longer than one thought it would, thanks largely to the American customers who guessed that the names of C. Fry and E. Evans must spell culture. It was not frankly a happy engagement, and apart from the money I was glad when it was over. At the end of the run, when business had sunk very low and Dame Edith, I think, had caught sight of me doing my stomach exercises at the back of the stage during one of her big scenes, they started dishing us out with a lot of free seats. On the Sunday before we closed, Mr Harold Hobson advised the readers of the *Sunday Times* that there were only eight more opportunities of seeing the classiest entertainment in London. The box-office was besieged, we did the best week of the run, and the management tried to get some of the free tickets back, which all goes to show that the Press *does* make a difference.

The most recent occasion on which I was asked to take over was in *Lysistrata*, that very old Greek comedy, whose plot depends on that ancient jape, men's dependence on women. It is described as diversely (or was apropos of the last production) as "the best anti-war play ever written" or "the bawdiest comedy ever", and one of its principal jests is to show gents in the highest state of sexual excitement. In the American Dudley Fittes translation, every other line has a *double entendre,* and in spite of the shortness of the play (it lasted well under two

Success Strikes Again

hours with songs and dances) it was a joke that palled on some people. Yet my mother (who is very wise) thought it charmingly done and nowhere near as dirty, dear, as *Tunnel of Love*, and unfortunately added that I was "outstanding", which was the sort of word that appeared constantly throughout the play. I always find other people's reactions to saucy plays very confusing, and must mention in passing that Mr Stewart Granger and I (and I'm not name-dropping more than usual) sat po-faced throughout *Roar Like A Dove*, by which we were deeply shocked, while around us middle-aged ladies had fits, and young ladies roared like lions. I'm no Criterion, as the Winter Garden Theatre almost certainly said to the Lyric, Hammersmith. (Haven't, luckily, thought of that sort of joke before.)

Anyhow, there I was, dressed in a sort of toga with an owl on my head, playing the Magistrate in the revival of *Lysistrata*. It had opened on Boxing Day, 1957, at the Royal Court, and I did not join the company until it transferred to the Duke of York's on February 18th, 1958. It opened very quietly, with little or no advance booking, until one night there was a demonstration from the gallery during the daring but comparatively disarming love scene. It started with cries of:

"Filthy."
"Disgusting."
"Take it off."
and rather quaintly,
"Give us some real drama."

These interpolations were followed by a shower of leaflets imploring the audience to write to their M.P.s and tell them to get the Lord Chamberlain to stop licensing disgusting plays like this. The leaflets were beautifully printed and apparently thrown down by three young men who left the building hurriedly. Needless to say, Mr George Fearon, our publicity gent, was round like a whippet, and we made front-page news the next morning with an immediate and splendid reaction in the

"I Know the Face, but . . ."

box-office. One or two of the more sceptical members of the company vouchsafed the opinion that the leaflets had been printed on the private presses of the English Stage Company, who were presenting the piece, but whoever had done it gave us a three months' extended run.

It was an exceptionally happy time for me, and like *Figure of Fun* I would have been quite content if it had run for years. Not that my part was a rewarding or interesting one, but it was a delightful and stimulating company, headed by three ladies about whom I have always been pretty potty, viz. the Misses Joan Greenwood, Natasha Parry and Patricia Marmont. In fact, it was only because I had known them so long that I essayed the role. It was apparent that they would never speak to me again if I didn't play it, so I thought I'd better get the money and risk them not speaking to me AFTER I'd played it. It was a large and extremely versatile cast, and the play was directed by a Greek gent called Minos Volanakis, who had a quicksilver brain and great charm. Unfortunately (for me) the transfer of the play coincided with his desire to reproduce all the songs and dances. So it was fairly difficult for me to get a word in edgeways at the dear old Chelsea Community Centre, where we rehearsed, and I actually had to play my last small scene at the dress rehearsal, having never what is called "Practised" it. However, my rendition of this part of the play galvanised the rest of the company into such looks of astonishment and/or horror that the audience failed to look at me.

The leading lovely ladies shared a dressing-room which seemed like a branch of Fortnum and Mason's. The food provided was sensational, flowers were always in evidence, and a strong smell of garlic, mixed with lilies of the valley, permeated the room. There were two radios permanently switched on to Continental stations, and litres of red wine to get us all into the mood, and I spent very happy hours there. And that was my

Success Strikes Again

last stage experience to date, and who knows when or indeed if I shall tread the boards again.

Although it is not, as the film jargon has it, strict continuity, I shall insert here details of a strange but successful experience I had in 1950, when I was asked to be in a play by W. Shakespeare, Esq., and you might have thought that my previous experience with the Bard would have precluded my even considering the proposition. But unfortunately I have a total inability to say "No" on the phone to any dear chum. So when the blower went and it was Paul Scofield asking me to be in something called *Pericles* I was clay in his hands.

"What's *Pericles*, Paul?" I asked.

"It's a play reputed to be by Shakespeare," replied Paul, "and you'd be jolly good as the Pander."

"I'll only play it if it's a Giant one," I said, "and even then you will have a lot of trouble with the costumiers, finding a skin big enough."

Paul said it wasn't that kind of a Panda, and anyhow the director, John Harrison, would like me to play the King of Antioch as well, and wouldn't it be an interesting double? and could he tell Harrison that I'd do it? and we'd get some very good tucks-in during rehearsal, and I said, "Yes, of course, Paul," and that was that.

The performances were to take place in the Rudolf Steiner Hall on two successive Sundays in July 1950, and were to be presented under the auspices of the Under Thirty Group. A lot of the artistes engaged didn't exactly come under that heading, but the whole thing was to prove a stimulating and enjoyable experience, which is more than most Sunday night perfs. are.

John Harrison, now I think in TV after a very notable few years as Director of Nottingham Repertory, had been an actor at Stratford when I got the S.,[1] but he obviously didn't hold that against me. He'd married Daphne Slater, the Juliet of that

[1] Details of s—k in Chapter viii.

"I Know the Face, but..."

season, who was going to play the hapless Marina in *Pericles*. Others in the company were Beatrix Lehmann and Mary Morris. Miss Morris was to play the part of the Chorus, which till recently was always played by a very old man. The casting of Mary and later Edric Connor, in the role have been revolutionary experiments which have indeed come off. Mary, one of the most talented and neglected actresses of our stage, had very definite ideas about what the Chorus should LOOK like. She arrived at the drill hall off Baker Street, where we were rehearsing, with a big envelope under her arm and sat down beside me with a conspiratorial air.

"Think I'll get away with this?" she asked, withdrawing a very highly coloured design from the envelope. I had a brief dekko and pushed it back into its hiding-place.

"Have a bash, dear," I said encouragingly, but I was anxious to see John Harrison's reaction to what the Chorus were to wear in their interpreter's opinion. They were to wear a gent's smart evening dress with black tights and a splendidly embroidered codpiece. It was actually a wildly over-exciting and imaginative conception, but I thought the spirit of Mary Baker Eddy, if still hovering over the Rudolf Steiner Hall, would leave for foreign parts forthwith. John Harrison went a bit pale when shown the design, and I saw Mary in deep conclave with him, using those oh! so beautiful eyes to telling effect. She returned to my side with a wicked gleam in them.

"THAT's no good," she announced, "but he says I can wear an ordinary lady's evening dress."

Shortly afterwards she disappeared to play on tour in *If This Be Error and* only reappeared on the Sunday of the production, when she created a fairly striking impression by being dressed in an absolutely transparent net dress which would have packed the building for months on end. She looked quite wonderful, and her haunting voice and appearance held the audience spellbound.

Success Strikes Again

The dress rehearsal was full of surprises even without this vision, and the scenes at the Rudolf Steiner Hall early that Sunday morning were remarkable. The little theatre is not wildly well equipped for dressing-rooms, and there were in fact only three usable, which is not quite enough for fifty-odd performers. Paul and I arrived nice and early into ours, so that we could carry out a rather difficult operation known as "Boling". It funnily enough has nothing to do with bowls, boll-weevils or balls (at least, not in this country), and means that you cover yourself in some brightly coloured fluid which makes you look as if you lived in sunny lands. It is v. difficult to "Bole" oneself because of the back problem, so Mr Scofield and I had made an arrangement, but we were a little put out to find, on our arrival in the dressing-room, about five young ladies lying fast asleep, or dead, on the floor.

We decided to ignore them, as we were informed that they had been working all night on the scenery and costumes and were therefore only dead-tired, so we left them where they lay. We stripped down to our pants and started the gruesome job of applying the "bole". Just as we had got really into our stride, one of the young ladies woke up, took a quick look at us "boling" and fainted dead away. It was not really a very good omen, and we got her removed as quickly as possible to a less dangerous locale. We then hurried on with our business before there were further casualties.

After I had been covered in brown paint, I put on my first costume for the role of the King of Antioch. It was a regal panoply of dark blue with enormous weights of jewellery attached to it. It was also unfortunately still wet, and when I removed it to become a Pander, I found that I looked like a Pict in Woad, if you know what I mean. It was all very tricky, because then I had to put the bole over the woad, and by the end of the day I looked like, but I fear didn't smell like, an apple and bilberry pie. It also, I think, contributed to a tiny

"I Know the Face, but . . ."

error that I made on the first Sunday. As the Pander I wore a smock shirt which came down below my knees, and had to sit cross-legged on the floor with the Bawd (Beatrix Lehmann, brilliant as usual). It was pointed out to me afterwards that, as I wasn't as lovely as Mary Morris, it would perhaps have been wiser to have worn SOMETHING underneath, and wasn't it lucky that it was a Club production and not a public performance, under which category my performance came.

There were some fairly fascinating people in the cast, and as the shipwrecked sailors and the brothel ladies wore a minimum of clothing, members of the cast, to say nothing of the members of the Under Thirty Group, got their money's worth. I had a scene with Paul at the beginning of the play when I tried to present him with a present of my daughter in order to curry favour. My daughter was v. beautiful and was called Dagmar Wynter and got in our line of sight a bit. We were both immobile owing to being wedged into seats (and in my case stuck to the seat with woad, etc.), so that I cricked my neck trying to see round Miss Wynter. At that time Miss Wynter was doing everything possible to shape a career for herself and was one of the most photographed ladies in the business; she often went to first nights and *premières* with the most elaborate hair-do's. She is now known as Dana Wynter, is a zonking great film star, and jolly good luck to her.

Others in the cast were a couple of brothers called Sinden (one was Donald), John Bennett, a talented young actor, with whom I was to share a dressing-room years later during the endless tour and almost non-existent run of Anouilh's *Restless Heart*, and two gentlemen who played chess ceaselessly in our midst throughout the performance, which gave a wrong atmosphere of relaxation, and as one of the players was deaf, it made ordinary conversation about the work in hand difficult. Above all this, I remember P. Scofield's superb, non-fussing and unselfish, gentle personality, which spread calm and confidence

Success Strikes Again

over the hysteria and seeming chaos. His leadership did not prevent him from giving a remarkable performance, which was rightly praised to the skies by the critics. There is no doubt that we would have reached a wider audience if Paul had not been committed to throw endless Rings Round the Moon at the time.

Chaper VIII

A FEW FABULOUS FLOPS

EVERY actor has been involved in at least one failure during his career and I have collected a good few in the last twenty-five years. Some of them were deserved, but every now and again one was in a play which had great merit, but no one seemed frightfully anxious to pay the money to see it. This is always dispiriting, particularly if the reviews have been good and there is no visible reason for its inability to attract the customers. For the actor it presents a problem, as he has to keep up a façade of pretending that it is all going to be all right even to his nearest and dearest, because only in this way can he keep his morale going. He is automatically plunged into an orgy of theatrical *clichés* like:

"It's picking up after a slow start";
"It's building gradually";
"Business is bad all round this week";
"The Ideal Home Exhibition (or the Motor Show) will help tremendously";
"Wait till the weeklies (or monthlies) come out."

You see, it is a show-business impossibility for a play to be doing badly because no one wants to see it. It must either be because the weather is too hot, cold, windy, muggy, rainy, or because there has been too little publicity or too much. It is probably caused by it being Lent, Ascot, just before Christmas, just after Christmas, everyone's away, "it's dead round the West End", and so on and so on, but the fact remains that people will get to the shows they want to see if there is petrol rationing, a bus strike or, let us face it, rocket-bombs falling like confetti.

Another reason given for failure to attract, is that the show

A Few Fabulous Flops

is at "the wrong theatre". But I think it would take an H-Bomb to dislodge *Salad Days* with its all-star cast from the Vaudeville, sometimes classed as an unlucky theatre. Other "unlucky theatres" include the Winter Garden, where *Witness For the Prosecution* ran for nearly two years, and the Princes, where one cannot get seats for love or money when the D'Oyly Carte Opera Company beat the hell out of Gilbert and Sullivan at regular intervals; and I cannot believe that the Fortune Theatre, which even taxi-men pretended not to wot of in days gone by, has regretted the presence of the enormous company in *At the Drop of a Hat*.

I will readily admit, however, that a well-placed theatre can turn a near failure into a reasonable success by attracting the "passing trade", and the Criterion Theatre is ideally situated for this sort of thing and I personally thought a lot of people ended up at *Waiting For Godot* thinking it was Piccadilly Circus Tube Station, particularly on foggy nights. And it is certain that any actor longs for his play to go to one of the following houses, all of which have an aura of success about them: the Haymarket, New, Wyndham's, Globe, Lyric or Apollo.

In my quota of flops, pride of place must be yielded to *The Boy David*, which played at what was then HIS Majesty's Theatre. It was J. M. Barrie's last play and had been written for Elisabeth Bergner, about whom the distinguished playwright was besotted, and I could not understand anything more easily. Quite apart from her enormous talent, she was the reincarnation of many a Barrie character. Her eternal youth and radiant face would have made a wonderful Peter Pan, but the biblical David was to prove a sad mistake.

We were first scheduled to open in the spring of 1936, and Cochran, who was presenting the play, had arranged an impressive array of talent. Augustus John was to be the designer, and William Walton would compose the incidental music. To

"I Know the Face, but . . ."

support Miss Bergner, he had engaged Godfrey Tearle, Sir John Martin-Harvey, Leon Quartermaine, Ion Swinley and Jean Cadell. Hangovers from *Escape Me Never* (besides Mr Quartermaine) included John Boxer and myself and the entire stage management from that piece. H. K. Ayliff, of the Birmingham Repertory Theatre, was to direct. The publicity was fantastic, and Cochran, who never believed in doing things by halves, made us rehearse behind locked doors in the wilds of Walworth in a not very converted Parish Hall. There was a general atmosphere of reverence and mystery about the whole thing that made us all whisper and creep about, which I found a bit spooky. It was all a bit mystifying, as I found on inspection that the play was totally different from the general conception as conveyed by the Press. It was principally a naïve domestic piece with little or no action, apart from the slaying of Goliath. Yet there was a dramatic power in parts of it, particularly scenes between David and Saul, which showed a master's touch. But the thing as a whole lacked cohesion and the casting of Bergner as David was little short of a major tragedy. In spite of her improved English, one felt that the portrayal could not be acceptable to the British Public.

After about ten days' rehearsal, we were quite suddenly told that Miss Bergner had appendicitis and the whole production would regrettably have to be postponed indefinitely. So we all said farewell to the dear old Walworth Road and I, for one, thought we'd never meet again; but in the autumn the whole enterprise was resumed, though with a change of director. This time we had Komisarjevsky in whom Bergner had tremendous faith, and quite naturally after their triumphant partnership in *Escape Me Never*. I was pretty keen on him myself, with his wicked smile and great sense of humour. Back in the Parish Hall we found very little changed and there was still rather too much reverence about.

Sir James came down and had a poached egg on toast at the

A Few Fabulous Flops

ABC, and we were all pretty frightened of him. It was not without cause, for he did not at first like the opening scene in his play as brought to life by Robert Eddison, Basil C. Langton, Eric Elliot and myself as the brothers of David. It was an almost impossible scene in which we wrangled and I made terrible jokes. My first line was "I call the world to witness that there is a piece of flesh in Eliab's bowl", which took the curtain up and really should have made it descend immediately, as the tentative way in which I spoke it was not likely to inspire confidence in the customers. Sir James was deeply displeased by the way we all played it, and at one period I was on the verge of being asked to leave the building, saved once again in my career by the intervention of Miss Bergner. The author's main complaint (he was a bit deaf) was that he couldn't hear his own words, so Mr Komis told us all to speak up, and after bellowing our way through the next rehearsal in terror, it became the author's favourite scene and he made us do it very often. He couldn't quite understand what Komis was aiming at and was not, I think, a very easy author to have around the place, but for the magic and pleasure he has brought to the theatre we must never cease to be grateful.

Before leaving for our try-out in Edinburgh we had a nightmare dress parade. After the whole cast (there were many extras for the Philistine fight sequence) had trailed back and forth across the stage for several weary hours, I heard Mr Komisarjevsky exclaim in a loud voice to Mr Cochran and the author (in the stalls): "Only one thing is clear. Bull must be clothed"; so another smelly old skin was added to my wardrobe. We were due to open at the King's Theatre, Edinburgh, on Saturday, November 21st, 1936, and we went up two days early for a couple of dress rehearsals, one of which was never finished, though we went on through the night. The advance publicity, to say nothing of the booking, was enormous, and as the Scots capital wished to honour one of its most distin-

"I Know the Face, but . . ."

guished sons, the castle was floodlit and seats were put up to 21s. for the first night. Miss Bergner, as usual, had managed to avoid the Press, and any information the latter received was at the hands of the two boys playing and understudying the part of Jonathan. One was Bobby (now Robert) Rietti and the other Kenneth Connor, now the well-known comedian. I kept quiet as a mouse in some nice digs with John Boxer and viewed the whole thing with gloom. I was not having an easy time with the Prophet Samuel with whom I had rather a lot to do in the play, mainly because Sir John Martin Harvey would not concede that I had any name at all after six weeks of rehearsals, and though I called him "Sir John" with great reverence, he would not speak directly to me and would merely ask Komis if "the stout gentleman" could move a bit farther downstage. This was lowering to the morale. But both Mr Tearle and Mr Quartermaine (with whom I played picquet a good deal) were charming, and after all there was always Miss Bergner at whose feet I was still in hopeless adoration.

The Edinburgh first night was a curious experience. Although the audience was friendly and attentive, it was quite obvious that they were disappointed and the evening seemed interminable. Barrie had decided at the last moment not to come, and there was a general air of anti-climax about it all, rather like an unsuccessful rocket-experiment. The reception at the end was lukewarm, and Judith Furse (who had assisted Komisarjevsky on the production) and I went and dined rather grandly at the Caledonian Hotel with my brother Anthony, who had turned up on business. The menu included "Délice de Sole Elisabeth" and "Biscuit Glacé Bergner", which I fear was a fairly accurate description of the evening. I was flabbergasted the next day to read in a Scottish gossip column that, owing to the reverence of the occasion, the company had been too overawed to celebrate at the Caledonian except for a minor member of the company, which put me in my place.

A Few Fabulous Flops

The criticisms the next day were respectful but non-committal, and for the next fortnight we played to packed houses who saw a different show every night. We rehearsed continuously and whole scenes were omitted at some performances and then put back the next night. The part of Goliath was sometimes seen but not heard and then not seen but heard. There was an episode where Saul's Little Thoughts came to Life with some young ladies playing the title-roles, and this scene was wisely withdrawn from regular consumption. But I readily confess that there were some unforgettable things in the production and at times Elisabeth was intensely moving and there was a pictorial piece of magic that I shall never forget. This was when, after David's fight with Goliath and a very noisy general battle scene, there was suddenly dead silence, and from way backstage a tiny figure appeared dragging an enormous spear behind her. Komis had lit it all superbly and Godfrey Tearle was magnificent as Saul. Unfortunately, after his disappearance in Act 2 there was a far too long whimsical scene between David and Jonathan, which had no tension and sent the audience away baffled and disappointed.

I think it was improved by the time we left Edinburgh and we were to open at His Majesty's Theatre on December 14th, 1936. There were reports of an unprecedented library deal and the excitement before the first night was tremendous. But although the donkey on which the Boy David made his (or her) first entrance behaved impeccably on this occasion (at Edinburgh he or she had done the lot on the first night), the waves of dislike and even hate that came wafting over the footlights were unmistakable and very frightening, I know I have never felt it before at a first night, and it was my first taste of the fickleness of public adoration. The idolisation of Elisabeth Bergner had changed overnight for no apparent reason. She was still obviously a great artist in the right setting, she had behaved with great dignity throughout, and yet suddenly the phrase

"I Know the Face, but . . ."

"she's always the same" became general. The terrifying thing is that she never regained her popularity in this country, and heaven knows what we have missed.

The reviews were very bad indeed and the library deal story must have been a myth, as the audiences were thin, even over the supposedly festive season. After five weeks it was announced that *The Boy David* would be withdrawn the following Saturday. As frequently happens with this sort of disaster, a stampede started at the box-office and the mounted police were called out on the last day of all. I am sure we could have run through the spring, but Cochran had lost faith and both Bergner and Barrie were heartbroken by the play's failure. Elisabeth was quite wonderful through all this, but I fear Barrie was never the same again and he died not very long after. The play is sometimes revived, but is a sad epitaph to his life in and for the theatre.

The next "flop" in which I appeared was not nearly as spectacular as *The Boy David*. It occurred after war was declared and they decided, as anti-Nazi propaganda, to revive a violent but effective play by Elmer Rice called *Judgement Day*, which dealt with the Reichstag Fire Trial. It had actually had a moderately successful run the year before and it was not really a very good idea to re-open so soon even at Pop Prices (6s. to 1s. 6d.). The first night was on November 21st, 1939, at the Phoenix Theatre, and the large cast were paid basic salaries of either £10 or £5 a week, according to reputation. I was paid £5 a week. It was very well directed by Murray Macdonald, and Freda Jackson and Glynis Johns (then a tot with tremendous talent) were magnificent in it, but the business was quite sensationally terrible and we played the piece twice daily, for some unknown reason.

My part was that of Kurt Schneider, a not at all thinly veiled caricature of Van der Lubbe, who was the scapegoat for the Reichstag Fire. It was a showy part and the sort of thing I am

A Few Fabulous Flops

very keen on. I was in the witness-box or court throughout and was drugged to the point of dottiness. I kept muttering sentences like "Vimmen, vimmen, I 'ave 'ad menny vimmen" which meant "Women, women, I have had many women". I didn't exactly underplay the role, and used to try to wake up some of the sleepier members of the cast by letting out a shrill scream when they were least expecting it. All this sort of caper led my mother, who had come to a matinée with, I think, my Aunt Sara to plunge headlong from the theatre into the street during the second act muttering, "To think I gave birth to that"—a remarkable tribute which I should have inserted in "Spotlight".

We were all of us actors on what is known as "sharing terms", which meant that, if we played to over a certain figure, our £5 and £10 were automatically increased for the week. I was unaccountably chosen to act as the actors' representative, which ensured that at any rate I saw the returns every night. After we had been playing to mere handfuls of people, suddenly there was a performance at which people were literally hanging out of boxes. The cast sparkled with joy, some of the sleepier members of the court woke up, and it was only when I got the receipt sheet from the front of the house that I realised it was only a wicked optical illusion. Instead of the £300 we had expected, there was £28. It was heartbreaking to tell my fellow buskers, and it was small comfort to know that the management had crammed the place with European refugees, who of course were thrilled with the play.

I don't remember much else about the run, except that a young gent called Jon Pertwee guarded me on the stage, and one of the lady witnesses' knickers slowly descended one matinée in the box, which cheered us all up a bit. We actors are simple folk. I left the play because I had been asked to appear in a film and the director did not think it entirely worth while to engage an actor who had a matinée every day.

"I Know the Face, but . . ."

Since the war I have been in rather more successes than flops, I am happy to say, but one play stands out in my memory as unique, in that it was a failure which gave me intense pleasure and enjoyment. I am referring to a play called *The Man With Expensive Tastes* which I cannot believe many of you saw. I think, on looking back, that it must have been very remarkable to view, and appealed to a wide range of those who actually caught it. Mr Ken Tynan often refers to it and Philip Hope Wallace once put it on his Recommended List, though I fear not for the usual reason. Several of my more distorted friends saw it twice, and Michael Gough followed us on tour and many a time stopped the action with his loud guffaws from the back of the stalls.

I had had rather a bleak time and was as usual in penury when Henry Kendall, who was to direct it, gave me the play to read. I was to play Monsieur Onyx, the head of a ring of forgers, most of the time disguised as an old clergyman. The description of the character is described in the published play: "He has long, sleek, curling white hair, carefully parted, which retains a touch of its original gold. You feel that it is probably a wig, because the rest of his face is singularly smooth and hairless. He has black kid gloves on his hands and a light white scarf twined round his neck. He wears tinted spectacles, so that his face has a strangely impersonal appearance. His voice is suave, but there is an occasional whip to his words which is rather exciting." I read this first and was fairly fascinated, but it was my agent, Laurence Evans, who finally persuaded me to do it, because he peeked at the end of the play where Monsieur Onyx gets his come-uppance. The Corsican lady who is in love with "the man with expensive tastes" says "Cretin" to Monsieur O. Then, as it says in the script, "She bends and whips the little dagger from her garter. It seems as though a flash of light passes between her and Mr Onyx. The latter's pistol clatters to the floor; he clutches convulsively first at his throat,

A Few Fabulous Flops

then at his head. His white wig falls to the ground, and a youngish man spins slowly round and drops dead on the conservatory threshold."

My agent, and supposed friend, asked me who I thought would be right to play the "youngish man". I took the play home and was absorbed by the intricacies of the plot. The main character was an elegant gent called Sylvester Ord, who liked to indulge himself in cigars, smoking-jackets and exotic plants like the obscurer forms of gloxinia. In order to afford indulgment in these tastes, he had to hypnotise himself into forging cheques for an organisation known as "The Ring", which was run, I am happy to repeat, by Monsieur Onyx, wig and all. He could only forge PERFECTLY if he was in a self-induced coma, and to complicate matters he caught his hand (the operative and forging one) in the door of a safe at the end of the second act. But I suppose if he had not met with this accident, there would have been no third act, and this was truly the highlight of this remarkable play. With his damaged arm in a sling he was able to hypnotise his daughter Sandra into the gentle art of forgery, and this she carried out superbly, and all would have been well had it not been for the interfering private enquiry gentleman (American) who seemed to travel about the house at whim.

That was the rough plot, and I decided to play Monsieur Onyx as I had no alternative employment and no money. The piece had been written by Edward Percy and Mrs Edward Percy. Mr Percy had scored many successes with such notable plays as *Suspect* and *Ladies in Retirement*. These he wrote with Mr Reginald Denham. Then he wrote *The Shop at Sly Corner* by himself. Afterwards he married Mrs Reginald Denham and they wrote *The Man with Expensive Tastes* together. The play was presented by Jack Gatti, the lessee of the Vaudeville Theatre, who, finding his theatre dead empty in the middle of summer, was desperate and instructed his manager to dig out

"I Know the Face, but . . ."

the last play done at the Q Theatre with only one set and which was a reasonable proposition. This turned out to be *The Man with E.T.*

After I had agreed to do it, I was sitting in the manager's office when I noticed the proposed lay-out for the posters. It read "George Curzon, Philip Stainton and Blank in *The Man with E.T.*" I realised that I was now Blank and that they must have scraped the bottom of the barrel to find an actor to play him. As a result I stipulated in my contract that I must not be "starred", as I have noticed with the years that if you go below the title, "They" (public, and above all, critics) do not think you as reprehensible or as responsible as when your name is in front of the play. I went to the bottom of the bill preceded by a large "AND".

We only had three weeks to get it on, and although we cut it and changed a lot, it still appeared a bizarre offering to me. Most of the cast, however, seemed to take it all dead seriously with the notable exception of the young gent playing the detective. I noticed that he could hardly get through the bit where he discovers that I am wearing a wig.

"Say, Padre, is that a toup?" he naïvely enquires, and I have to explain that I am wearing it because fish-poisoning had left me with "chronic eczema of the hands" (black kid gloves explained) and "alas no hair" (toup *ditto*). The role of the American investigator was played by Maurice Kaufmann, an instinctive and talented performer who has yet to have the break he deserves, but I am bound to admit he saved my life during the run and tour of this extraordinary play. His sense of humour and general support were invaluable and we forged a friendship that I value highly. Though Henry Kendall helped a lot by removing some worrying bits, I was still left with some tricky scenes. One was when I summoned my coloured chauffeur (Munch by name) and he brought me a massive copy of the Prayer Book, in which was concealed a revolver. I was handi-

A Few Fabulous Flops

capped too by the fact that, as I was playing a double part, I kept on having to change my personality, and as I find it practically impossible to sustain one character part at a time, let alone two, I ran into a bit of trouble. The only concession I found myself willing to make was to wear a pair of pince-nez to signify that I was PRETENDING to be a benevolent old clergyman at a certain time. Needless to say, I kept on forgetting which I was, and anyhow the pince-nez kept on falling off so that the resultant perf. was nowhere near as polished as the pince-nez would have been if they had had any glass in them.

We staggered on and came to the dress rehearsals, when further drastic alterations were made. One of them was wise and concerned a scene where I had to imitate Mr Kaufmann's American accent on the phone, which was so unlike the original that it confused even me. It was a horrid time and I was in blackest despair. The first night was on July 23rd, 1953, and I had unwisely given my friends a rough *résumé* of the plot. This meant that there was a full turn-out. Robert Morley brought his family (including his lovely mother-in-law Miss G. Cooper), Richard Burton bought a box, and Richard Leech and his wife were others who came to try to stop my probable lynching. The author popped into my dressing-room before the play and gave me a small ivory cross which he wanted me to wear on the stage. I decided not to, and hastened into that lovely little Catholic church in Maiden Lane to pray that there would not be a holocaust.

Strangely enough, the audience behaved impeccably, and only at the very end, when I had to pretend that the dagger had gone into my throat, did their decorum vanish as I fell to the ground inside the conservatory, and the curtain calls were so quick that I don't think the audience realised that it could be over, or that they had actually witnessed what they had, during the past two hours. I am bound to admit that my friends seemed to have enjoyed themselves hugely and Bob Morley bet

"I Know the Face, but . . ."

me £5 that it would run six months, a debt he has never paid, but then, neither have I paid him the money I owed him for betting that *The Little Hut* WOULDN'T run six months, which only goes to show how wrong everyone can be.

The notices were universally damming, though the cast escaped lightly, and the critics were pretty witty about the whole affair and suggested that it would not prove an entirely wasted evening. The first few performances were reasonably well attended and the returns, I am afraid, compared favourably with those of *Goodness, How Sad!* seventeen years previously at the same theatre. But it was patently obvious that we were not going to beat *Chu Chin Chow* in our staying powers, and indeed were to run only three and a half weeks. But everyone with a remotely perverted sense of humour made their way to the Vaudeville Theatre, and I had frequently to close all the windows of my dressing-room in order that the ribald mirth and general post-play hysteria should not permeate the upper regions of the building. There was a ghastly evening when I caught Mrs Richard Burton and Miss Claire Bloom far too near the stage, stuffing handkerchiefs into their mouths, and I thought about to have two fits.

After the last night Mr Gatti gave us all a tuck-in, which was generous of him, and we all departed severally and I thought that was an end of that; but no, a few days later I was asked to go on tour with it. It was intended to play the Birch Circuit, which sounds more exciting than it was. The phrase refers to a series of theatres purchased by a Mr Ralph Birch, who had suddenly entered the theatrical arena and was just as suddenly to disappear from it. The towns involved included Brighton, Folkestone and Wimbledon for a start, and Luton and Swindon were thrown in for good measure, two dates which intrigued us all considerably as no one we knew had played at them for centuries.

A Few Fabulous Flops

We had luckily caught Mr Birch during his prosperous era and I received a salary far in advance of my deserts. It was a very happy tour, and as it was still summer, the seaside weeks were delightful. Maurice Kaufmann and I had a whale of a time, being involved in such diverse pleasures as the Ladies' Hockey Championships at Folkestone and the Swindon fair. There were one or two changes in the cast and a lot of the props supplied by the Gatti family were withdrawn as the receipts fell. Except at Brighton, where we played at the tiny Dolphin Theatre, business was disastrous; and at a matinée at the Alma Theatre (yes, really), Luton, we played to £3. But curiously enough, apart from a shaky Saturday night at Swindon, the sparse audiences took the play dead seriously, which I fear is more than a large percentage of the cast did by this time.

There were some excruciatingly funny moments, as when at Brighton the stage was so small that the conservatory became like the Marx Brothers' cabin and I found no room to do my death-fall without sweeping all the gloxinias and at least two of the cast on to the floor. Then there was the time when the manservant is about to bring on the tea. Usually there was no noise and I, with superb artistry, suggested:

"I think I hear tea."

On this particular occasion the actor playing the servant dropped the entire tray with a clatter that echoed through the theatre.

"I THINK I hear tea," I announced, and left the stage and the rest of the cast to cope with the situation as best as they could.

Luton was our last date and we were able to commute from London; and I was genuinely sorry that the whole thing was finishing. After the first night we never saw the authors again, but my advice to you is, if you ever see a bill announcing the arrival of *The Man With Expensive Tastes*, to hie to the place of entertainment with all convenient speed.

"I Know the Face, but . . ."

Lastly, in this saga of things not going quite right, I turn from fairly public catastrophe to a private fiasco. I am referring to the 1947 season at the Memorial Theatre, Stratford-on-Avon, in which I almost took part. It all happened after my disastrous plunge into theatrical management after the war with *Cage Me A Peacock*. Having sold most of the furniture, all of my shares, and borrowed from my friends, I wasn't exactly sitting pretty when Walter Hudd, at that time artistic director of Stratford, rang up and asked me if I would be interested in the idea of playing Sir Toby Belch, Caliban and one or two other parts in the forthcoming season. At first I thought he must be joking, or that some friend was indulging in some pretty poor taste, but I realised he was serious when he asked me to go to Hampstead to discuss it.

I could not understand why he had elected to think of me, as my only previous experience with the Bard was in the film of *As You Like It*, and my William could have given no hint of latent genius for verse. I was not even then thrilled by the idea, as I must confess the thought of being a Shakespearian actor has always bored me. I have tried to take in the beauty of it all, and have frequently been stirred by some exciting production or performance in one of the plays, but usually I stay clear of them, as to me the basic stupidity of some of the characters is irritating beyond endurance. Why, for example, doesn't King Lear realise what Cordelia is saying to him in that first scene, when it's as plain as a pikestaff to me and the rest of the audience that she is in fact v. keen on her father and that the week-ends he is planning to spend with the other girls are bound to end in disaster? And why for heaven's sake doesn't Olivia realise that the other lady is in gentleman's costume the whole time? And why are Romeo and Juliet so out of touch with the drug situation in Italy not to realise that one or the other has just taken an overdose and those fools Friar Laurence and the Apothecary are no help at all?

A Few Fabulous Flops

I suppose I am the one who is so stupid, but if I was directing a Shakespearian production (and you can thank your stars that this is never likely to happen), I'd make Cordelia have an impediment in her speech, and Lear wear a deaf-hearing aid which had gone wrong, and stop *Romeo and Juliet* altogether after that lovely first act. As for Viola, I would make her open her mouth while a deep bass voice said HER lines off-stage.

So for various reasons my heart sank at Mr Hudd's proposition to cloister me on the Avon for many months, but, being near bankruptcy and having literally nothing else on the horizon, it was madness to turn it down. I did, however, stipulate that by mutual consent at the end of two weeks' rehearsal we could part company with no umbrage and no money changing hands. I pointed out that I did not even know which play was which, and Mr Hudd said this was Healthy. In any case he was directing *Twelfth Night*, and we'd soon see which way the wind would blow. Actually it blew me right out of the Memorial Theatre, Stratford-on-Avon, but that is anticipating.

I started off with the best intentions in the world and a pretty nice company to boot. There were old friends like Robert Harris, Veronica Turleigh and Beatrix Lehmann, and a lot of young gentlemen destined to rise to the top: Donald Sinden and three embryo directors, Douglas Seale, Julian Amyes and John Harrison. Above all, there was Paul Scofield, simple, funny and a loyal and marvellous person who at that time had almost as big an appetite as I, which ended in us usually having two complete all-in lunches at the cafés in Holloway, where we rehearsed. It was bitterly cold and the practice hall belonged to Sir Donald Wolfit and was situated just opposite the ladies in Holloway Prison. It was none of it very cheerful, and Paul and I kept our fur gloves on most of the time.

At the end of my parole I spoke to Mr Hudd, who expressed himself delighted with my efforts and said he had no reason for alarm and that I must overcome my diffidence. I thought I

"I Know the Face, but . . ."

lacked confidence and was not really getting to the bottom (in this case the stomach) of the part. As somebody so wittily put it, I was more like a Burp than a Belch. However, I was not getting in a panic, as by now I had started rehearsing in the opening production, which was to be *Romeo and Juliet* and in which I was enacting the part of Montagu (old). This was being directed by Peter Brook, and the rehearsals of this one were very exciting indeed. Peter Brook is a short genius who stands bolt upright throughout a production, so that there is never any question of the actors having an excuse for feeling tired. I love working with him, because he gives me great confidence and some of his results are breath-taking.

Soon we were bundled out of Holloway to the Avon for final rehearsals and I stayed at a nice little hotel called The Fold, which was run by some people called Lamb, so we were all able to have some jolly japes of an agricultural nature, what with my name and all. I had stayed there during the tour of *The Lady's Not For Burning*, and this time the Lambs gave me the run of the kitchens in the evenings, which was madness. However, I could not afford to stay there the whole season and I searched high and low for a flat, cottage or room without success. I am here to say, with prejudice, that I personally loathe Stratford-on-Avon and this feeling is, I hope, totally unrelated to what follows. The atmosphere of old Tudory and brass ornaments brings my bile to boiling-point, and I did fancy during my short stay there, that no one in the town seemed frightfully keen on the actors, who are largely responsible for bringing the shop ladies and gentlemen their revenue. There hangs over all an air of smugness and self-satisfaction that cloaks the place like a polythene bag.

Having got that off my chest, I am returning you (as they say on the radio) to the rehearsals of *Twelfth Night*, during which I did sense a slight feeling of exasperation emanating from the producer towards me. He had realised by now the unlikelihood

A Few Fabulous Flops

of my (*a*) mastering the Viola da Gamba, (*b*) fencing with any accuracy or lack of danger to my fellow artistes, and worst of all (*c*) singing in tune. I am unfortunately tone-deaf, and though I don't necessarily stand up when they play "Land of Hope and "Glory" (thinking it's the "God Save" as my mother does), this deficiency is no help when you have to sing a "round" like "Hold Thy Peace, I prithee hold thy peace". I did count aloud between the lines to give myself assistance, which made Mr Scofield (Andrew Aguecheek) laugh, but I don't think Mr Hudd was best pleased. But I did TRY, and Feste (Dudley Jones) wrote it out on sheet music, which I pretended I could make head AND tail of. But that scene became rather shot with tension, partic. after I started to boggle at tickling Malvolio under the nightie.

But I must have been extremely unaware of the true state of affairs, because it came as quite a shock one March morning when I received what can only be described as The Sack. It's never pleasant for an actor to get the "s", and was a crushing blow, as I had made all arrangements to spend the summer and autumn away from London. I was also frightfully angry when there was a quibble about the compensation I thought due to me. I left in a rage, mitigated by the sweetness of the Scofields and other members of the company, and only recovered my sense of proportion on the train from Stratford to Leamington Spa the following morning. In my carriage I found a lady called Denne Jilkes, who is the nicest thing about Stratford. She dispenses warmth, music, voice lessons, hospitality to all and sundry, feeds the hungry and lodges the homeless, and I had met her briefly before getting the "s".

She knew about my *débâcle* but did not refer to it. She was carrying two large boxes covered in canvas, which had arrived by post that morning, she told me, from her doctor son who was on a Polar expedition. She slit them with a knife and revealed some intimate parts of a whale's fossilised anatomy.

"I Know the Face, but . . ."

She was hugely delighted with her presents and I felt suddenly much better. We laughed long and loud together, and I told her that she and her whale had probably changed my life. I felt years younger at throwing off the Avon yoke and returned home in high fettle. I did, however, have the curiosity to attend the first night of the London season of the Stratford-on-Avon company and would like to think that the series of mishaps on the stage that night, in a production of Walter Hudd's, were totally disconnected with my despicable private thoughts.

Chapter IX

B TO Z FILMS

As most actors know to their cost (in every sense of the word), the gap between the first feature film and the small budget movie is immense, and as it has become an economic necessity to appear in the latter, I think it only right to tear the tinsel off this branch of the industry. For several years now I have lurked about in the background as a sinister character in "B" films and other ghastly opuses, and I know what I am talking about. Though a lot of these enterprises have had their funny sides, the results have been frequently hair-raising. I want to make it clear that there are honourable exceptions, and every now and again one has the luck to be in a little film, which by sheer talent of the director, turns out to be very worthwhile.

But for the most part they are shot at enormous speed against the clock, and there is no time for direction, subtlety or, quite often, rehearsal. There are even occasions when whole characters are altered a few minutes before a scene and brand-new dialogue is shoved under your nose practically as the camera is turning. Everyone suddenly behaves as if the Day of Judgement is being shot immediately afterwards. Contrariwise the popular idea that "such a lot of time is wasted" could not be less correct under these circumstances, and there is practically no "sitting-about", not that there would be any chairs to sit on, should this unlikely opportunity arise.

One of the more bewildering examples in which I took part was *Salute The Toff*. Such was the apparent demand for films about "The Toff" that they were shooting two at the same time, with the same characters involved. So far, so fairly normal; but I must report they were using the same sets as well, only with

"I Know the Face, but..."

the furniture changed round. The scripts were different, I admit, but it was foxing for the artistes and in particular for poor John Bentley, who was playing The Toff in person and constantly had a good deal to do in both films and had to switch sometimes from one to the other in the middle of a day. He got very tired indeed, and when a message came through to the studio to say that he had had a breakdown I, for one, was not remotely surprised, though it turned out that he was referring to his motor-vehicle.

I was as usual playing a crook, and had to slap my mistress (Shelagh Fraser) in the face to get the film an "X" certificate. There was quite a droll afternoon when I had to make my escape through a window. Unfortunately they had placed under the window one of those arrangements on which you unpack your luggage. You've probably guessed that my flat in *Salute the Toff* had been an hotel bedroom for *Hammer the Toff* earlier that day, and this article of furniture was having a busy day. It was also equipped with the usual slits in the wood and we did not have any time for rehearsal, as it was nearly a quarter to six. On the word "Action" I made for the window and caught both my feet in the thing and was so firmly wedged that I had to take it through with me. I am bound to say they did re-shoot this scene.

All the dialogue I have to speak in this type of film is interchangeable, and my part usually starts with a close shot of my big face puffing at a cigarette and saying this sort of thing:

"Diamonds, my dear Wainwright, are always a responsibility (*puff*) unless you can dispose of them satisfactorily" (*puff*).

The similarity between the characters I play and the words that I speak in these films is enhanced by my limited wardrobe. If you have only two smart crook's suits, it is jolly difficult to look frightfully different, though I am helped enormously by the generosity of Mr S. Granger, who has kept me in shoes, overcoats and heaven knows what else since I don't

B to Z Films

know when. Every time he leaves these shores for America, he tends to shed his property like manna, and I fear I hover around like a vulture. His most notable contributions have been a super camel-hair coat and a saucy American mac. Unfortunately, the news about these acquisitions spread round the Rialto, and chums, who were appearing in "B" films of like calibre to the ones in which I got involved, begged, borrowed or stole these garments. The camel-hair number suffered most, as the majority of my friends wished to wear it in its natural form, viz. double-breasted. This didn't suit me at all, as I had turned it into a single-breasted affair for circumstances over which I should have some control but haven't. So chums' wives and/or girl friends had busy times sewing off and on buttons to suit the occasion. It was, I suppose, at one time the most familiar coat in the business, and one day I wore it in the morning and handed it over after lunch to Maurice Kaufmann, who was appearing at the same studio, though in a different film. With the help of the wardrobe mistress, it was thus able to appear in two roles on the same day, a sartorial record.

Luckily Mr Granger's shoes did not fit anyone except Mr Granger and me, but very distinguished his old crocodile numbers looked in close-up, for an episode in the TV series "Dial 999". They were observed walking down Shaftesbury Avenue at the time, and all three of us had an agreeable few days round the West End. I had been engaged to play the part of "Blowey" in the Scotland Yard film, and there were happily very few lines to master. The series was produced by that dynamic figure Harry Alan Towers, and this particular episode was directed by Alvin Rakoff, a temporary fugitive from TV. My first call was for "11 o'clock in the car park by the Phoenix Theatre off Charing Cross Road", and that's as cosy an hour and location for a film engagement as one can imagine. Certainly for one of my circumstances and address, as a number

"I Know the Face, but . . ."

19 or 22 omnibus would deliver me direct from my home to my place of employment.

It was a lovely summer's day and I chatted gaily away with my prospective fellow-artistes, who included such upholsterers of the business as Robert Beatty, Sydney Tafler and Peter Reynolds. I was cordially greeted by my director, who seemed surprised to see me there. Later in the day I discovered that he didn't know I was "Blowey", but had thought that I was on my way to somewhere like Foyles and had dropped in to say "Hullo."

I was not needed during the morning, so I spent most of it in some of the more disreputable coffee-houses in the Soho area, but in the afternoon I dusted Mr Granger's shoes in order that they and I could chase Mr Tafler in and out of St Martin's Lane, and later down Shaftesbury Avenue. Mr Reynolds, a small actor called Mr Wade, and I were the pursuers, and Mr Tafler affected a limp for the film. He limped very fast indeed and Mr Granger's shoes and I were hard put to it to keep up. At the beginning of one shot Mr Tafler had indeed almost disappeared round a corner and a tart came up to us and asked what we were doing. We said that we were filming and she asked if she could be in it too and we said but of course! and she must follow Mr Tafler, which she did, and Mr Reynolds, Mr Wade and I followed her. Mr Rakoff said that wouldn't look quite right on the screen and would we please do it again, this time without the tart.

The Shaftesbury Avenue sequence was much more tricky, as there was to be a concealed camera at the back of a van, which would shoot Mr Tafler and his pursuers while all parties were in motion. Since it was the rush hour, the number of people one knew who seemed to be walking down the street at the same time was legion. As they were not appearing in a film, they seemed to be put out when, after greeting me effusively, I was only able to say, "Eff off. I'm filming" delivered out of

B to Z Films

the corner of the mouth. As we neared Piccadilly Circus things got very hectic indeed. I don't know if you've ever tried to cross to Swan and Edgar's from Shaftesbury Avenue AGAINST the lights, but I can't advise it as a method of exercise unless the death-wish is over-developed. Rarely have I been so petrified, a state not helped by the conviction that any moment I might be arrested for careless walking.

The van, which had covered the expedition, stopped outside Austin Reed's, which was civil of it, as I popped in to buy a jumbo pair of pants. Throughout the film I wore some dark glasses which turned out to be a Good Thing, as the *News Chronicle*, reviewing the attraction some months later, said it had caught "tantalising glimpses of Peter Bull lurking through dark glasses". It was quite a jolly experience altogether, and I regretted that I was unavailable to take part in others of the series of which this episode was the "pilot" film. I did, however, contrive to get into a similar enterprise called *Martin Kane, Investigator*, in which I played a foreign scientist (on Their side of course). At one point I was handed a deadly secret formula with ingredients which I promised to "test in my lead chamber". Later I was shot beside my lead chamber, but in one of the takes got caught on its handle by Stewart Granger's pullover, and THAT had to be re-shot, as it looked a bit funny apparently.

A few years back I was in a series of remarkable film-making projects produced by a pair of brothers called Proudlock, most of whom had been educated at Eton. They had entered the industry in their twenties with enormous enthusiasm, not much money and some pretty startling ideas. I liked them immensely. My first assignment was Chief Menace in a film called *The Six Men*, which was to be shot in ten days. The cast were invited to a reading of the script in one of the Proudlocks' flats in Hyde Park Square. I remember that we had a very classy tea served in a splash of Georgian silver, which seemed out of keep-

"I Know the Face, but . . ."

ing with the proposed budget. I finished my part in the studio in two days flat, which amazed everyone, including myself. I never saw the film, but I understand it was not entered for any of the major film festivals.

My next job for the Proudlocks was an afternoon's work making faces for a film called *Smart Alec*. One of the bros. had rung up the day before to say they were in a bit of a quandary and could I lend a hand. They had practically finished the film, and had to be out of the studio the next day anyhow, but had discovered the running time was not long enough and could I fill in some of the gap by appearing in close-up as a prosecuting or defending Counsel in a Court Scene. I said yes but of course, if I could do the week-end shopping first and cadge a lift back from Shepperton. They agreed and that would be six guineas and I said no ten and we settled for eight and I had an agreeable afternoon hamming my head off and I didn't see that one either.

The next Proudlock prod. in which they so proudly presented me was a more than off-beat version of *The Second Mrs Tanqueray* which was to be filmed simultaneously by at least four cameras, thus saving time and expense, if they didn't bump into each other continuously. On the whole this method worked smoothly, though actors in trances came in for some rough handling. We all tried to keep our eyes wide open, but it was largely a case of "Sauve Qui Peut". Miss Pamela Brown played the title role, Mr Hugh Sinclair played Mr Tanqueray and I took the role of somebody called Misquith, the mere mention of whom sent Mr Tanqueray into hysteria. He seemed deliberately to pause between the two syllables of my name, but I did get my revenge by calling him Audrey instead of Aubrey, in the up-to-then famous dinner-table scene. I do recall a cat coming down a chimney during a ten-minute take which didn't help matters, and the film was shown at Notting Hill Gate one Sunday but I was abroad at the time.

B to Z Films

The Proudlocks then bought a disused cinema in Barnes which they first turned into a studio cinema and then a cinema studio or *vice versa*, but they never asked me to appear there. *The Second Mrs Tank* had been directed by my friend Dallas Bower who had been so kind to me and was the one who had cast me as the boxing champion of the world. He has given me all sorts of work to do through the years and he is a stimulating and interesting personality. One of the oddest enterprises he wedged me in was a film of *Alice in Wonderland*, in which all the parts were played by puppets except those of Alice and rather surprisingly Queen Victoria, Prince Albert and Disraeli, who appeared in a prologue, which mysteriously was shot in the South of France.

To supply the voices for the puppets a very comprehensive gathering of artistes were assembled. They included Felix Aylmer, Jack Train, Pamela Brown, Stephen Murray, Joyce Grenfell (wonderful as the Doormouse, I remember) and myself (fair as 4th Gardener). The recordings took place in the tiny Merton Park Studios and very enjoyable they were. The film, however, never reached our screens publicly, owing to some jiggery-pokery about the rights and the Walt Disney production of the same subject.

Sir Douglas Fairbanks has been a great boon to all us struggling actors in this country and his TV films gave employment to thousands. I managed to get into two of them. The first was rather classy and was directed by Roy Rich. It was a political satire about an unnamed country (Russia) and starred Bernard Lee, Greta Gynt and Robin Bailey. It was called *Border Line Case* and is constantly thrust on the viewer when he, she, or it, is least expecting it.

The other one was a bit joky as far as I was concerned. It starred Sir Douglas himself, who was very cordial to me and went as far as commanding a close-up of the inside of my mouth as I screamed the place down (I was being killed at the

"I Know the Face, but . . ."

time). I personally didn't feel the shot would have a wide appeal to the viewer and it possibly explains why this particular film doesn't seem to have reached my four-inch screen yet, though it may have filtered through to yours.

It was called *Now and Forever*, and was the sort of film where a young American serviceman meets a young Wren, Wraf, or At while wandering round a picture gallery or ancestral home. They are of course looking at a picture of some ancient forebears, who look exactly like them and whizz bang! we are back in the seventeenth century with the Roundheads and Cavaliers at it hammer and tongs. During most of this part of the action the young lady (played by Miss Muriel Pavlow) was locked up in the Tower for Political Reasons and I was the head Turnkey, if that's what it's likely to be called. I called Miss Pavlow "Mistress Barrington" a good deal and was beastly to her. I had two difficulties to surmount. One was that I kept thinking of her as the "Young Mrs Barrington", which is a modern play by Warren Chetham-Strode, and the other was that I had to stomp about with the largest bunch of keys ever seen on a turnkey. So far, so good; but the trouble was that the keys made such a clatter and a jangle that the director made me hold them until I was stationary, if you follow my meaning. The general effect of this restriction was to give me an impression of not having a single hernia but a double one. As I approached Sir Douglas and Miss Pavlow, it was fairly difficult for them or indeed me to keep a straight face.

Oh yes, I have had some happy times making TV films, and by far the pleasantest was when I appeared in an episode in a series called *Dick and the Duchess*, rather haphazardly I thought, but perhaps it is only because I have such a common mind. They were produced by a very glamorous lady from France, called Mme Nicole Milinaire. I came back home to my flat one day to find a rather cryptic but intriguing message written on my pad by my daily. "Ring Mrs Millionaire at

B to Z Films

the Berkeley Hotel," it read. I fixed an appointment *via* her casting director, Maud Spector, and put my best suit on for the interview. It was a Saturday morning, and I found myself sitting opposite one of the most attractive ladies I've ever seen, who didn't quite fit in with the usual conception of a TV film producer. She wanted, she said, a list of the best restaurants in and around Chelsea, and Miss Spector had told her that I was reasonably well-informed. It seemed a novel qualification for getting a part, but I was more than willing to supply the info.

After I had shown my French off a bit, with frequent references to "ratatouille" and "Lapin Gaullois", she did ask me if I'd like to play an official in the R.S.P.C.A. in a small scene in her series. She would be so honoured, she said, and I kissed her hand and nearly fell down the lift shaft at the Berkeley and waited anxiously for the day's work. It turned out to be a monologue and on the telephone at that. It took place in a tiny office and I was called for 11.30 (a civilised time, if ever there was one). I met the charming American director, Sheldon Reynolds, who looks like a film star but wisely isn't, and he told me I wouldn't be required till after lunch. I pottered around the M.G.M. Studios where a lot of my chums were working on *Barnacle Bill* and had a hilarious lunch in the restaurant.

I was called to the set about three and gently rehearsed in my role by Mr Reynolds. He seemed quite happy about the proposed rendering and said: "I think we'll shoot it now. Bring on the other actors." As I had thought it was going to be a monologue, I was faintly surprised when the following entered, either being carried or under their own steam, so to speak: a couple of parrots, a vulture, two goats, a great many mice, a monkey, a rabbit, four cats and a dog or two. I decided to play up to Mr Reynolds and pretended that it was exactly as I had visualised the scene. It was rather difficult to sustain this attitude when they attached a goat to the desk, put a not frightfully happy monkey in a cage one side of me and plonked

"I Know the Face, but . . ."

the fattest white rabbit I've ever seen on top of a lot of papers in front of my face. All the camera crew and bystanders were in hysterics, but I managed to keep a dead-pan face and indeed enjoyed myself hugely. Grasping the telephone receiver in one hand, I dislodged the rabbit from time to time with the other in order to consult my papers. I did not forget to say "Do you mind?" and "Thank you" to it when the circumstances demanded. I then spasmodically fed the monkey with bananas, absent-mindedly eating them too. We did it in one take, and if we'd done it a hundred times, the animals and I could not have given better perfs. I was out of the studio by four, after one of the most enjoyable hours I've ever spent in a film.

But animals aren't always so co-operative, and I was once in a peculiar film about greyhound-racing called *The Turners of Prospect Road*, which most of my friends (so-called) found unforgettable. It was all about a taxi-driver (Wilfrid Lawson) who owned a greyhound, and I played the leader of a gang who tried to dope it. The film was made for practically nothing, as we shot most of it either at the White City or at a track down at Clacton or Clapton or some such place. I started off with an off-beat Cockney accent which vanished a quarter of the way through the film. It was an unpleasant film in which to be appearing, as you were apt to be handed pages of new script every morning, which is the sort of thing that makes you lose a Cockney accent anyhow. The leading dog got very ill indeed and had to be made up for the big race which was the climax of the film. It also had to be given an enormous start in the Greyhound Derby in order to complete the course at all. (Query? Can dogs sue for libel?)

It was a depressing atmosphere to film in, as we had to dress in the loos of the race-tracks and everyone was anxious to finish the film as soon as possible. Jeanne de Casalis was brought in to play a Mrs Feather character, which struck a novel note, a lot of people had hysterics from time to time,

B to Z Films

and one of the principal actors disappeared shortly afterwards to prison for forgery. I just went to a psychiatrist. The interior shots were done in the small Carlton Hill Studios, which counted as "Location" for some unknown reason, so we were taken in full make-up to a restaurant round the corner and given a 4s. 6d. all-in lunch. The film made, I am told, a small fortune for the company, who didn't pay my psychiatrist's bill, although it was largely my difficulties with the lines that drove me there.

The problem of line-remembering is an extremely serious one for the actor. Although in *Goodness, How Sad!* the audience always laughed at the scene where Peter Thropp recounts the sort of questions laymen always ask actors, like: "How do you know when it's your turn to speak?" the line is more penetrating than it appears. The actor himself usually knows when it's his turn to speak, but he quite often can't think what he should say. There are no golden rules, and the greatest actors of all have suddenly found themselves bereft of words and in need of a prompt. It frequently happens in the middle of a long run, and for nights on end the actor dreads the moment and knows he's about to "dry", and can do nothing about it. Luckily the phase passes, and then all goes smoothly until the next crisis. But I think this is part of the reason why actors should be highly paid; it is the nerve strain and suffering that makes it such an insecure job and at the back of most of our minds is the fear of hearing somebody use the dread phrase about oneself: "Oh, he has difficulty with his lines, poor chap."

I used to go through such miseries before first nights and TV transmissions that I stood in my dressing-room over the basin, unable to be sick, but just making terrifying noises. Not very comforting or attractive for any busker sharing the room with me, but a lot of people are taken that way. I used also to get into the bad habit of having a photographic enlargement of the script in front of my eyes, which meant that, instead of

"I Know the Face, but . . ."

concentrating on what and to whom I was speaking, I was thinking, "This is the page where I have three long speeches. If I get to the bottom of this one I am home and dry." This did not make for a convincing performance, although I suppose it's better than not thinking at all.

With films it is different, because one knows one can always do it again if one has made a muck-up, but the temperamental film director can make one lose every shred of self-confidence, so that one becomes a gibbering lunatic. After a certain number of takes they might just as well call in another actor, or preferably another director. I can still remember after twenty-five years a speech which I had difficulty in remembering at the time. It was in *The Beloved Vagabond* and I had to make it to M. Maurice Chevalier (no less). The film was being shot simultaneously in French and English, and in order to earn an extra four pounds I had said that I spoke fluent French. It was not quite fluent enough apparently for the director, who danced about in rage as I got more and more English.

The funny part about it all is that if the task seems superhuman and almost impossible, some miracle happens and one gets through with comparative ease. I recall fixing to play a leading part in a film one morning, going down to the studios that afternoon, getting a script and shooting quite a lot that day. It was a film produced by (guess whom?) the Proudlocks, and we completed it in $3\frac{1}{2}$ days and it was shown at the Marble Arch Pavilion (deceased) as a second feature aptly called *Strange Cargo*.

But to go to the other side of the picture (if I may use the phrase). Every now and then a dream job occurs, in which one not only has very few lines to memorise, but one is suddenly transplanted to an exotic location, where quite often one stays at other people's expense for weeks and indeed months on end. I have not had many of these opportunities, but the ones I have had have been fraught with interest. For years I had been

B to Z Films

deeply jealous of chums who were always leaving for Cannes, the Costa Brava, Rome, or at worst the Outer Hebrides, to appear in films, but I was suddenly engaged for one called *I'll Get You For This*, starring Mr George Raft. It was to be shot largely in San Remo, and I was to play the part of Max. I said "Snap", but was faintly bewildered, on tearing through the script the first time, to find no reference to Max at all. However, an intenser survey brought to light a night-club scene in which Max said:

"You're wanted on the phone, Signor Sperazza."

That was all Max had to say (in my script), and for the life of me I could not imagine why this scene had to be shot in sunny Italy. However, it wasn't my place to argue and I hootled happily off to the airport with my script, my bathing dress and my sun-glasses. It was April and beautiful, and I spent most of the time on the beach, mainly with a Hungarian adventuress. She had, she told me, lost all her money at the tables and would I be interested in having her as a mistress? I wasn't, as it happened, frightfully interested, but she did vastly amuse me with a constant tissue of lies and splendid romances with crowned and recently uncrowned heads of Europe. She was always very hungry, and I had to smuggle food out of my hotel a good deal.

But far more fascinating was Miss Renée Houston, who was the first person I saw on my arrival on the set, which was the actual gaming-tables of the Casino. She had been a great friend over the years and for a decade or so I had followed her round the Variety Theatres of England in order to catch her act.

I honestly thought she was the funniest woman in the world and I was potty about her. After I had caught her the first time (her husband Donald Stewart partnered her) I forced all my friends to share the experience and in a short time the front row was solid with her supporters, whenever she appeared anywhere in London. It was never remotely the same act and

"I Know the Face, but . . ."

she relied on her customers for backchat. Her brain was so quick that she could deal with any heckler, latecomer or disapprover in seconds, but I am afraid on the nights we were there, her material was far too specialised for the ordinary audience.

I was at the first night of a straight musical show in which she appeared called *Love Laughs*. It was at the Hippodrome and Renée scored one of the biggest personal successes anyone has ever made in a musical comedy. She was the talk of the town and even James Bridie wrote a play for her. Playing the romantic lead was a rather arch lady whom Miss Houston started imitating the third week of the run, which threw the plot out of gear, but once she had begun, she couldn't stop. Her mimicry is superb, and French, Italian and gibberish are child's play to her.

I remember Sir John Gielgud telling me how he had done the Balcony Scene from *Romeo and Juliet* with Gwen Frangçon-Davies at the Coliseum in a Variety programme. The Houston sisters followed them and did a replica of the scene, which convulsed them and the audience. I saw them both (the Houston sisters) as the Babes in the Wood at Birmingham. With Douglas Byng as the Governess, this was the most adult pantomime I have ever witnessed. The next Christmas entertainment I caught her at was *Robinson Crusoe* at Brighton, where she seemed to be playing Girl Friday. The afternoon I arrived, she'd just sent the Parrot home as it had a temperature. Since it had no understudy, the management were a bit cross and were not inclined to agree with what was written outside Miss Houston's dressing-room door. It said quite simply: "The Nicest Woman in Show Business."

I have seen her in many strange settings. One such was the Dominion Cinema, where she was sandwiched between two rather bad films as a "bonne-bouche". The audience were dazed by her act and her sole accompaniment was a rather sad gent on the Mighty Wurlitzer. At the end of her act, the afternoon I was there, she finished to tepid applause, led by Judith Furse and myself, who had loyally supported her twice that day. She tripped daintily forward.

"Thank you, thank you, thank you," she said, "from the bottom of my heart. Do all come out to tea"; and turning to the Mighty Wurlitzer she added: "You come too and bring your organ."

She could be merciless with her audience. Anyone she caught looking at their programme during her act she would seize on immediately.

"The name's Houston," she would shout, "Renée Houston. You won't know me, child, but your father would. AND your grandfather. Sweetheart of the Forces in the Boer War I was, and proud of it."

During the war she toured the provinces with one of the most extraordinary entertainments I have ever seen. The entire Houston family were in it and it played in some bizarre places of pleasure. I caught it at a cinema in Clifton, and unwisely sat in the front row; she stopped dead in her tracks on her first entrance. Advancing to the footlights, she yelled at me:

"Peter Bull, if you follow me any further I'll put the police on you. I'm telling you straight I've had enough." She burst into floods of tears which caused me to slink away to the back of the theatre and confused the audience, who thought they were in the middle of a back-stage drama. Later in the war I made the error of visiting the Shepherd's Bush Empire, wearing my sailor-suit with "H.M.S. Hesperus" on the cap-ribbon. Miss Houston's act was punctuated with references to the "Wreck of the Hesperus", which the audience didn't entirely understand.

The stories about her are legion. It is said that she always had laid down in her contract during her Variety days that she must never have nudes appearing in the same programme. This

"I Know the Face, but . . ."

clause was apparently broken in a Northern theatre. A posing act was on the same bill, but only for the first two performances. Miss Houston lay in the wings on her stomach during the second, with a peashooter poised daintily between her lips.

"Not that I have anything personal against the dear child," she murmured as she blew through it.

She always took the keenest interest in the acts of those appearing in the same bill, and I shall not easily forget an evening at the Brixton Empress when the gay Irish Boxer-singer Jack Doyle was sharing the top of the bill with his current wife, Judith Allen, a film actress. Theirs was a curious act, as it consisted mainly of Mr Doyle lying on his back pretending he was on a bicycle and Miss Allen doing totally incomprehensible scenes from films in which she had appeared. Miss Houston followed them smartly, and lay on the floor pedalling. After some exercises she announced shyly that she would like to do a few scenes from HER films. I shudder to think what the atmosphere was like backstage that week.

But Brixton is a tidy step from San Remo, and I should not have digressed so much, but Miss Houston has always been one of my favourite diversions and is to me the best example of the survival of talent in the theatre. She has in her time faced every known setback, she has been "discovered" in every medium of the arts, only to be shoved back to Square One, but has emerged recently as a stage and film comedienne with depth and attack, and taken her place as one of the foremost character actresses in the country.

As I have always followed her career with the keenest interest, it was nice to be able to creep up behind her in the Casino and say:

"Ah, there you are. I wondered where you'd got to." It turned out that her gentle dear husband (Donald Stewart) had a largish part in the film and she had accompanied him for the ride. It was a hilarious time for me, and for the work part I had

B to Z Films

to walk up a cliff once and down a street twice. I didn't utter and even on my return to a London studio I had several lovely lazy days as background before working up to the ordeal of telling Signor Sperazza that he was wanted on the phone. By this time my one line was the joke of the unit and everyone was kind enough to tell me how it should be delivered to best effect. I had bought a new pair of evening-shoes to go with the line. They cost me 16s. 6d. in a curious sale at Peter Jones's, which I thought reasonable. The day dawned and I rehearsed the shot, sick and faint with the worry of it all. At the end of the scene the Sound Gent said coldly to the director:

"I think it would be better if Mr Bull removed his shoes. I cannot hear the lines owing to their squeaking." I played it in my stockinged feet, and still wear the shoes at every *soirée*.

The next foreign location I visited was North Africa. It was for a film called *Saadia* and was being shot in and around Marrakesh. The stars were Cornel Wilde, Mel Ferrer and the lady known as Rita Gam. I saw the American director, Al Lewin, at Claridge's, and landed the part of an Arab Chieftain. I was only given a page of dialogue this time, not an entire script. My part was one speech, which went as follows:

"Are we to interrupt the tax-collecting for such a trifle? One would say that Moha's accursed daughter were the manchild of a Caid on whose health the welfare of our village depended."

It was, as you can see, quite a mouthful, but I would hardly have thought it worth carting me out to North Africa just to say that. I never saw the film myself, but I don't think it did anybody much good, even Miss Wanda Rotha who played the lady witch-doctor. I was unfortunate enough to arrive right at the end of the film-making and everyone as usual had embarked on a strict economy drive. Otherwise I think I might still be there banging away about Moha's accursed daughter. One friend of mine, who was playing a French officer, got to his

"I Know the Face, but . . ."

line, "There should be a full moon to-night", at least three full moons after arrival.

I flew out to Casablanca on a Bank Holiday, after being in a TV play about Pontius Pilate. I was given a ticket only as far as Paris, as I was assured I would be met by someone at Orly airport from M.G.M. who would route me on and generally cosset me. Needless to say, there was no such character on a Bank Hol. and I was in a quandary. Although Easter in Paris tempted me, I knew I was already a day late owing to P. Pilate and they might not be best pleased. I phoned the M.G.M. office, who managed to square the booking dept. and I left with much misgiving on another aeromachine.

I arrived at dusk in Casablanca and was driven at breakneck speed to Marrakesh along a traffic-crammed road, stiff with the results of accidents. I clung on for dear life and arrived at the Hotel Mamounian severely shaken at 11. I was whipped straight off to the wardrobe dept. and was told I'd be needed in the make-up room at 6 a.m., so they were obviously making up for lost time. The next morning, in a pseudo-daze, I was made up by a dear man called Mr Frost who blackened my face, and after taking a quick look at the lovely gardens in the hotel I was transported to a tiny Arab village in the mountains where the shooting was to take place. Here there were just the thousand Arabs squatting on the ground and the Messrs Ferrer and Wilde. They were both friendly, especially the former, who was carrying exactly the same novel as I was. The Arabs just went on squatting and staring throughout the day. They were quiet as mice and a tidge sinister mice at that.

My director Mr Al Lewin smiled benignly throughout the day, but I did happen to notice that he wore a hearing-aid, which I imagine he switched off whenever the French assistants got over-excited. At any rate he retained a smiling and impressive calm throughout a day fraught with unpleasantness and hysteria. I just got through my piece of splendid rhetoric,

B to Z Films

though nearly on my knees from tiredness and the heat. I spent a lot of the afternoon discussing the theatre with Mr Ferrer, who was not taking *Saadia* all that seriously.

We finished about seven, and I was in the last shot of the day. Hardly able to move, let alone speak, I got back to the hotel, where there was a curt note telling me I would be leaving early next morning. This anyhow would have rendered me speechless with indignation, so my vocal condition remained static. I was livid inside, though, as I thought at least I might have been allowed one day in which to recover. But what really got what can only be described as my goat was the fact that the orders were couched in a fashion I hadn't seen since my service days. It gave the actor no chance to say, "I think I'll stay on a few days at my own expense," and just remarked, "Be ready to leave at 0700 hours. M.G.M. wish you a pleasant trip."

I stormed down to the Production Office, where I saw a Mr Goldschmidt, who was in charge of production. I said in a Blimpish way that I was not accustomed to being treated this way, that I would send in a full report to the authorities, and in any case had no intention of returning to my native land so soon. I had not quite decided where I would go, I continued, but I might look in at Tangier and visit the Vice-Consul. Would he kindly have my routing altered to enable me to stop off there? To my amazement he agreed to this and sent me to the Cash Office to draw my expenses. Whether by design or error the Cash Office seemed to think I had been out there one week and not one day, and I fear I did not disillusion them, which accounts for the fact that I was able to spend well over a week in Tangier, thanks largely to "Moha's accursed daughter".

Chapter x

WAITING FOR GODOT

It all began during that lovely, lovely summer of 1955; I was minding my own business and quietly enjoying the sun at the Oasis and Serpentine swimming-pools, when a phone call came from the Arts Theatre. A Mr Peter Hall wanted me to read a play called *Waiting For Godot*. He was away in Spain at the time, but had left word that he hoped for a speedy decision. Whatever the play was like, it needed time to consider the pros and cons, because although I was in my usual parlous state of penury, the prospect of a few weeks' work at the Club theatre didn't exhilarate me. You are (or were) paid twelve pounds a week and nothing at all for rehearsals (four weeks), though you were presented with a sheaf of tickets with which to purchase luncheon at the snack bar. An additional liability is that friends wishing to see the piece invariably have to get you to get them tickets, as you have been made an Honorary Member. If you are in a very popular play they rally round like flies and if you aren't frightfully good, forget to come round after the performance and pay for their seats. This is a double disappointment.

But, and it is a big But, some of the productions there have enormous prestige value and do one a lot of good professionally; for example, *The Lady's Not For Burning*, which only played for two and a half weeks at the Arts Theatre but was to provide me with the best part of two years' work. Contrariwise I have also played there in a sensational flop called *Second Best Bed*, which was the Coronation offering of the little theatre. A gentle satire on W. Shakespeare's courtship of the late Miss Hathaway, it incurred the wrath of critics and audience alike. We did appalling business with it although, just

Waiting For Godot

before one Saturday matinée, I popped my head inside the box-office and asked for eighty-four seven and sixpenny seats for that performance (meant as a joke actually) and the lady said: "I'm sorry, Mr Bull, we're sold out for the matinée."

I was frankly incredulous until she told me that the British Drama League had arranged for a section of its membership to come, and had booked the seats before the notices. Very rarely have I played to an angrier audience, who practically hissed their disapproval, and it was quite a relief at the evening perf. to play to our usual half-empty house, mainly composed of non-paying customers, or members of the Arts Theatre Club who could find no armchairs available in the lounge.

So on receiving the script of *Waiting for Godot*, I had one hit and one miss as precedent. I also found myself totally incapable of making any sort of decision after reading the play for the first time, which was in itself an extraordinary experience. I thought either the author or I must be potty, and yet even at first reading there was a hypnotic quality about the dialogue which could not be lightly dismissed. But I could not begin to understand what my proposed role (Pozzo) meant, and in consequence decided to turn it down, as I considered it pointless to contemplate playing a part through which I could see no daylight. I had hardly turned it down before I received a charming letter from Peter Hall asking me to reconsider the play and diabolically suggesting that I was ideal for the part. It was so cleverly phrased that I was completely won over to the idea, though even when I had agreed to have a shot at it, I stipulated that, if I felt unhappy in the part after a few days' rehearsal, I could leave. The fact that I felt unhappy months after playing it has nothing to do with this point. We were to start practising the first week of July and I looked forward to it with alarm and despondency.

The original cast was composed of Paul Daneman, Timothy Bateson, Peter Woodthorpe and myself. The only one I knew

"I Know the Face, but . . ."

nothing about was P. Woodthorpe, who was a discovery from the Cambridge Footlights Company and drove us all barking mad at the beginning. It was infuriating in my case (my silver wedding with the theatre had just been celebrated) to find an amateur actor with more talent than oneself, acting one off the stage, and his seeming confidence and technique struck an impertinent note. It was also a bit galling to discover that he hadn't yet made up his mind as to whether to go back to the University for his final year or continue to play with us. He was at any rate a "natural", and I've rarely seen such incredible promise. Timothy Bateson was fairly new to me, though vastly more experienced, and I remember him playing very old gents and young things at the Old Victoria Music Hall and with Sir Laurence and Lady O, in all those *Cleopatras*. As we were to remain tied to each other throughout the engagement, it was essential that we should remain on friendly terms, and in this we succeeded admirably and I found his acidity and wit helped me enormously throughout a depressing run.

Paul Daneman played Vladimir (one of the two tramps) only at the Arts and gave a wonderful performance, tinged with great compassion and simplicity. He was a tower of strength and a joy to work with. To complete the cast was a small boy, and the young actor playing this part had to be constantly whisked out of the theatre, when the "Dirty" bits were being spoken. He also had to be changed periodically, owing to the L.C.C. laws regarding stage children. The result of this was a caterpillar of young gents of varying talent and disposition. One with the face of an angel could be heard from one end of the theatre to the other hurling very adult epithets at his mother. Rehearsals started soberly, and I took an instant liking to the young director Peter Hall, who made no bones about the play.

"Haven't really the foggiest idea what some of it means," he announced cheerfully, "but if we stop and discuss every line

Waiting For Godot

we'll never open. I think it may be dramatically effective but there's no hope of finding out till the first night."

There was certainly no assistance coming from the author Mr Samuel Beckett, and looking back on the production, I'm rather glad he didn't put in an appearance till quite late in the run. The rehearsals were the most gruelling that I've ever experienced in all my puff. The lines were baffling enough, but the props that I was required to carry about my person made life intolerable. Aspiring actors are hereby warned against parts that entail them being tied to another artiste, as they will find it restricts their movements. As well as this handicap I had to carry an overcoat, a giant watch, a pipe, lorgnettes and heaven knows what else. The rope had to be adjusted continuously, so that I could pull it taut round my slave's neck, if possible not throttling Mr Bateson (Lucky was the name of the character). Fortunately there were long duologues between the tramps, so while they rehearsed on the stage proper, Master Bateson and I could have a bash in the Oak Room of the Arts Club, until complaints came up, via the head-waiter from the restaurant below, about the noise and general banging about. It was wonderful weather (always is during rehearsals), and at lunch time I used to grab a sandwich or eight and dart off to the Oasis swimming-pool. This brought back sanity with the chlorine and I was able to get through the afternoon. They were dreary days and evenings, as none of us, I think, dared to go out at night, owing to the necessity of getting the lines into our noddles. One of the main troubles was that an identical cue kept recurring every few pages of the script, so that it was remarkably easy to leave out whole chunks of the play. (We did, in fact, skip four pages on the actual first night at the Arts but, like fools, went back instead of pressing on.) In the second act I had to say "Help" about twenty times, a cue which didn't in fact help my fellow actors.

I found it frightfully difficult to get any sense out of my in-

"I Know the Face, but . . ."

tended characterisation, until the last week of rehearsals, when I suddenly decided to cheat and pretend Miss Margaret Rutherford was playing the role, which had the immediate and blessed effect of stopping embarrassing myself. It is a platitude to say that when an actor embarrasses himself, he is bound to embarrass the audience. I had noticed that my friends were clearly mortified at having to hear my lines, and Bob Morley had thrown the script from one end of his garden to the other, when I had unwisely asked him to take me through the part. The dress rehearsals were gloomy affairs and not relieved for yours truly by the physical discomforts of wearing a wig constructed of rubber, in the middle of a heat-wave. Owing to the author's eccentricity it was necessary for Pozzo to take his bowler-hat off at one stage of the piece and reveal a completely naked head. This was symbolic (the only explanation for the nightly torture given to me) and then he put his titfer on again. It was only for a second or two, but proved to be one of my major miseries. A firm of wig makers, Wig Creations Ltd., had constructed for me what amounted to a bathing-cap, which had to be encased in rubber solution. This caused an *impasse* when dry, owing to lack of air in the hair, and by the end of any performance there were several pints of not madly attractive sweat accumulated in the rubber wig, which made one feel as if one's head had burst. Later in the run I contracted a series of skin diseases as a result and had to issue a *pronunciamento*. The consequence was that a new type of bathing-cap was dished out, not so chic, as it had a few wisps of hair at the back, which meant that I did not have to seal off my head completely. The whole thing was pretty preposterous because, as Mr R. Morley kindly pointed out, the wig-join was clearly visible from Row K in the stalls. Make-up has never been my *forte*, and in this case the earlier I came in to do it, the more frightening seemed to be the result. I used to arrive some two hours before my first entrance in *Godot*, and by the time I reached the

Waiting For Godot

stage, the rubber started to come unstuck, which resulted in *ditto* for my performance. If I ever got held up by necessity or accident and got into the theatre late, I was always able to put on a superb make-up in ten minutes flat!

The first night was, I think, my most alarming experience on the stage (so far). I have a habit of comforting myself on first nights by trying to think of appalling experiences during the war, when terror struck from all sides, but the windiness felt on the Italian beach-heads and elsewhere was nothing to compare with one's panic on that evening of August 3rd, 1955, and why the cast were not given medals for gallantry in the face of the enemy is inexplicable. Waves of hostility came whirling over the footlights, and the mass exodus, which was to form such a feature of the run of the piece, started quite soon after the curtain had risen. The audible groans were also fairly disconcerting. By the time I had to make my first entrance (twenty minutes after the rise of the curtain) I realised that I was in for a sticky evening and I'm not referring to my rubber wig. The laughs had been few and far between and there was a general air of restlessness and insecurity around. I lost my head quite early on by inserting the rope, to which Mr Bateson was attached to me, INSIDE my coat sleeve. Knowing what I do now and how the audience were never surprised by anything that happened during *Godot*, I should have just said, "Pig, put my coat on properly, pig", which was the endearing form of address that I habitually used to my slave.

As it was, I spent the next quarter of an hour in a semi-hysterical condition, knowing that if I hadn't actually strangled Mr Bateson by the time he got to his big speech, it was highly probable that he would have to make it in pitch darkness owing to non-arrival at the position on which his spotlight was trained. As it was Mr Bateson's big moment, I hazarded a guess that he might not be best pleased. I gradually eased the rope up my sleeve in order to reduce the danger, but at the expense of

"I Know the Face, but . . ."

my performance, which had by now been reduced to a question of survival without having heart failure. I was blowing the audience out of the auditorium with the volume of my shrill voice—(quote Kenneth Tynan) "over-vocalisation" (unquote) which was the understatement of the year. But T. Bateson got his light, declaimed his gibberish and brought the house down with terrifying accuracy.

After this the audience were a little more attentive, and though an occasional groan or rudely upturned seat rang through the building, we got through without disaster. I pulled myself together in the second act and the Messrs Daneman and Woodthorpe were very moving indeed in the last scene of all. The curtain fell to mild applause, we took a scant three calls and a depression and sense of anti-climax descended on us all. Very few people came round, and most of those who did were in a high state of intoxication and made even less sense than the play. I slipped quietly away with the Scofields and Maurice Kaufmann, who had all promised to pick up the bits.

The notices next day were almost uniformly unfavourable, confused and unprovocative. We played to poor houses, but on the Sunday following our opening the whole picture was to change. We quite suddenly became the rage of London, a phenomenon entirely due to the articles written by the Messrs Tynan and Hobson in the *Observer* and *Sunday Times* respectively. One phrase quoted from each doyen of criticism was enough to send all London running to the Arts and subsequently the Criterion Theatres. Mr Hobson said, "Something that will securely lodge in a corner of your mind as long as you live", and Mr Tynan told his readers that "it will be a conversational necessity for many years to have seen *Waiting For Godot*." With no mock humility I have to report that Mr H. also said, "This Bull's bellow troubles the memory like the swansong of humanity," but I fancy Mr Derek Granger in the *Financial*

Waiting For Godot

Times was nearer the mark when he said I looked like a "vast obscene baby".

That Sunday night we played to near capacity and the whole trend of audience behaviour was to alter for the remainder of the run at the Arts. Gusts of laughter and tense silences greeted our efforts, and people started to come round to tell us what They thought the play meant. There were rumours even of a transfer, but in the meantime our run was extended. Mr Hobson mentioned the play every week in his columns, and we were suddenly informed that Mr Donald Albery, who owned the rights of *Godot* anyhow, had arranged with his father Sir Bronson Albery to take us to the Criterion Theatre. This was a real turn-up for the book, as this delicious little house is a dream emporium for the actor's wares from every angle. It has what is known as a marvellous "passing" trade, is easily accessible and a wonderful theatre to play in. The only disadvantage lies in conditions backstage, which is nobody's fault, but at first sight one might easily be in the sewers of Paris. It is chronically airless and there are mixed pongs coming from the restaurants and kitchens above. Owing to the smallness of the cast we were able to have a largish dressing-room to ourselves, and after a slight argument with Mr Albery about billing, I signed the contract.

I hoped it would sound a bit grand, that last bit about billing I mean. It wasn't actually and I merely happened to ask my agent to arrange that I should be billed after Hugh Burden, who was taking over the part of Vladimir from Paul Daneman who was about to go into the ill-fated *Punch Revue* at the Duke of York's. I didn't ask for neon lights or red letters eight foot high or anything, but Mr Albery said there was no question of order of billing, as he exercised the right to have the names of actors on the bills or NOT. He was absolutely correct and in order, but I did point out (through my agent) that there would be not much point, having performed anonymously at

"I Know the Face, but . . ."

the Arts Theatre, in doing *ditto* at Piccadilly Circus, the Centre of the World. We came to a midget *impasse* and I decided not to rehearse for a few days until things were settled. I popped off to the Oasis swimming-pool, while he made up his mind whether to replace me. Fortunately for me he decided against that and I returned browner, and I fear smugger, to rehearse.

We opened in the second week of September and were to run continuously till the end of the following March. It was the oddest theatrical experience of my life and had a nightmarish quality that is difficult to recapture in words. Both physically and mentally it was a disturbing play with which to be associated. The bleakness and sordidity of the set and the clothes, the spitting and drooling that formed part of the pattern, had a most depressing effect on me and I came to dread going to the theatre. I also found, as time went on, that I started to disbelieve in the merits of the play and to become more and more intolerant of the praise and importance that were bestowed on it in certain quarters. I got wildly bored by the endless banging-on at parties, in the street and particularly in my dressing-room. But of course it was all this *brouhaha* that helped to pay my rent for so long.

The High Teas on Saturdays helped a great deal. For me one of the nicest traits in Mr Donald Albery's character is his care of his actors' stomachs, and with a twice-nightly carry-on every Saturday (5.30 and 8.30 perfs.), he has instituted a splendid idea in his theatres, whereby a kind lady comes in and serves delicious cold-cuts and coffee between the two shows at enormous expense to Mr A. The actors can then lollop away to their dressing-rooms with a plate and make pigs of themselves. It was a bit tricky when friends came round between shows, but one could usually find a bone to toss to them. In any case I kept a widow's cruse of brandy handy, not only for myself, but for those customers stalwart enough to stay the course.

Waiting For Godot

It must be admitted that a lot of people didn't, and it was a remarkable thing to come on in the first act and feel a bungful house, only to return in the second to find a certain percentage of gaps in the theatre and the audience shrunk in size. Not that it was a great surprise, because those who had left did not attempt to cover up their movements. It was not just the banging of seats and slamming of exit doors, but quite often they would take the trouble to come right down to the footlights, glare at the actors and make their egress into outer space, snorting the while. Incidents were numerous and cries of "Rubbish", "It's a disgrace", "Take it off", "Disgusting", and I regret to say on one occasion "Balls", floated through the auditorium. There was one unforgettable night when, during the second act, the two tramps are alone on the stage cogitating about life as they were apt to do and one says: "I am happy," to which the other replies, "I am happy too," after which a gent in Row F shouted: "Well, I'm bloody well not."

At this point there was a certain amount of shushing, but the man would not be shushed and stood up and yelled at the audience: "And nor are you. You've been hoaxed like me."

A free fight ensued (well, fairly free; 15s. 6d. a head actually) and during a lull Hugh Burden observed quietly:

"I think it's Godot," which brought the house down and enabled our attendants to get rid of the angry middle-aged man.

But perhaps the drollest night was when I got my comeuppance. It had been reported to me by the stage manager that a party of eight had arrived rather late, and had made a good deal of noise sitting down in the front row. They were all in full evening dress with a fine display of jewels and/or carnations. By the time I'd been on for a bit I realised that they didn't seem best pleased by me or my performance. The muttering and whispering grew to a crescendo, until in a loud clear voice the dowager lady seated in the middle of the party said:

"I do wish the fat one would go."

"I Know the Face, but . . ."

I took a hurried look round at my fellow actors and decided that I had never seen a thinner bunch and guessed that she must be referring to me. I was a fraction shocked as, after a long and not terribly notable career in the service of the theatre, I have never actually been insulted DURING a performance. People have attacked me in the streets or in public transport, but never while I was actually doing it. I seethed inwardly with rage, but apart from glaring at the lady I was unable to make a come-back; luckily my beloved slave made handsome amends. As we were about to leave the stage, I shortened the rope which bound me to T. Bateson and he made as if to leap into the lady's lap, a threat which caused the entire party to leave hurriedly. Afterwards we were all filled with intense compassion and the milk of h.k., as it turned out that the party had arrived expecting to see a revue called *Intimacy at 8.30* which had vacated the Criterion Theatre a few weeks previously. Putting one and five together and realising the storm of criticism that would assail her at the end of the evening, the hostess had wisely decided to cut her losses.

Of course a lot of people were blackmailed into coming to *Godot* by the quotes in the Press plastered outside the theatre and in the newspaper columns. It was no good expecting to find "one of the funniest plays in London" if two tramps wrangling for a couple of hours on a stage, naked except for a leafless tree, wasn't your idea of a gay evening out. Then there were those who thought they wouldn't be asked out ANYWHERE if they hadn't seen it, thanks to Mr Tynan's pronouncement about it being a "conversational necessity". Sometimes I longed to stop prospective customers streaming up to the box-office and try and divert them to *Dry Rot* at the Whitehall Theatre, though I fancy a lot of them thought they had been seeing the latter anyhow.

But theatrical London did flock to it, and in consequence the piece did one's reputation a great deal of good, though a lot

Waiting For Godot

of members of the profession were not strong enough to stay the course. Early in the run my phone rang one morning and it was Mr R. Morley on the other end.

"Guess who was in front last night?" he asked.

"Boris Karloff," I replied correctly.

"AND me," he said, hurt. "At least, for the first act," he added. "But I told the people I was with that there was no point in staying for the second, as it was exactly the same apart from you being dumb in it."

I told him coldly that I was blind in the second act, and that I had troubled Mr Harold Hobson's memory "like the swan-song of humanity", but Mr Morley could not be tempted to return, and indeed his memory was so troubled that he used to ring me up periodically and mutter on the phone:

"I've been brooding in my bath, and it is my considered opinion that the success of *Waiting For Godot* is the end of the theatre as we know it."

Constance Lorne, a brilliant Perranporth graduate, came by herself one evening, and in the interval her neighbour turned to her and asked:

"What do you make of it?"

Constance, temporarily floored, opined that it made a change from all those ice-shows, at which the lady burst into floods of tears.

"It's my last night in London," she sobbed, "and they told me I HAD to see this."

Miss Lorne comforted her and packed her off to the Prince of Wales revue round the corner. During Motor Show Week we did sensational business, but the rush to the exit doors could not have been conducted faster than if it had been the twenty-four hours' race at Le Mans. One night after the curtain had fallen to no applause, a lady motorist rose to her feet and shouted to the world in general:

"You bloody suckers."

"I Know the Face, but..."

Not all of the criticism was vocal, and a lot of our unfan-mail came in with a twopenny-halfpenny stamp on it and sometimes with no stamp on it at all. There was a gentleman who wrote in to say that he didn't pay fifteen shillings and sixpence to smell Peter Woodthorpe's feet from Row S, and a lady who pointed out that her pipes were frozen, her drains refused to function, and that she'd come up with her daughter to take their minds off things and would we send her twenty-seven shillings by return.

Of course not everybody felt like this. Hordes of people thought that it was "absolutely wonderful", "a great treat", "gloriously funny", "heartbreakingly noble", "took one out of oneself", or "it was just like life". I thought them "absolutely wonderful" too, because it meant that I was paid for several months longer than I had ever dared to hope. But even this type of customer could be alarming, because they either sat spellbound in respectful silence or laughed their heads off in such a sinister way that the actors thought that they must have forgotten to adjust their costumes. And it was worse when they came round to the dressing-rooms after the play to tell us what the play meant. It was far too late for that sort of thing anyhow, and it didn't help me at this stage in my portrayal to learn that Pozzo represented Fascism, Communism, Lord Beaverbrook, Randolph Hearst, Mussolini, James Joyce, or rather surprisingly, Humpty Dumpty.

It was all a very great strain and preyed on our nerves, and it is easy to understand why one of the actors who played my part on the Continent went barking mad and had to be locked up for a bit. Considering everything, it was amazing that I only contracted laryngitis, colitis, dermatitis, and found my friends saying that they had noticed a CHANGE in me, not, I gathered, for the better. I do realise now that I was very irritable and nervy for many months and that this state was entirely induced by "my work".

Waiting For Godot

The author left his Montparnasse lair and visited us round about the hundredth performance and proved to be shy, modest and not frightfully helpful about the meaning of his play. We got the impression that he didn't care for the London production a great deal. He gave us a party, where we were all rather rude to him, but he took it in good part, and left for France after telling us that he didn't think the pauses quite long enough. We told him that if they were any longer, not a customer would be left in the building. Our Christmas arrangments (usually a cheerful sight to the actor when posted outside the theatre) were announced, and included just the ten performances in Christmas week. It wasn't, we felt, a madly Christmassy or festive play, or indeed, absolutely the attraction that the kiddy-winks would insist on being taken to, but it was no good arguing with the bosses on this subject. It was suddenly broken to us, however, that we were going to have a relatively new production incorporating a lot of Beckett's ideas.

This news came to us by a carrier pigeon and we could not believe that there was a vestige of truth in the rumour. But a rehearsal call went up on the board, and we were instructed to report every day during the week before Christmas which didn't quite fit in with our Christmas arrangements. It was then that I saw red, which (let's face it) never suits an actor of my nomenclature, and I suggested that it might be wiser, before embarking on a series of rehearsals, to engage an understudy for Mr Burden and Mr Bateson. Their current one, Mr Roderick Cook, was about to leave our establishment in order to play in *Listen to the Wind* at the Arts Theatre. Both the Mr B.s were a bit peaky in health round about this time, and it seemed ludicrous to us that they were not what is technically known as "covered", with a cast of only four men and a boy.

However, nothing constructive was done about it, though it is fair to say that auditions were held, but no one was apparently suitable, and on Christmas Eve the inevitable occurred.

"I Know the Face, but . . ."

T. Bateson had an impacted wisdom tooth, and his poor dear face was swollen up to balloon size. He played several perfs. in great pain and discomfort, but it was out of the question for him to play any longer. And so there we were, up the creek without an understudy. It was an impossible part to learn in a day or indeed weeks, but by a freak of chance, the Arts decided not to give a performance on Christmas Eve, and Roderick Cook was released to play Lucky, and very good he was, too.

But far worse was to follow. I was having a sensational tuck-in on Boxing Day when the Stage Director phoned to say that Hugh Burden had been taken away in an ambulance, and he would be obliged if I would come to the theatre as soon as poss. I got there, I regret to say, rather ebullient and be-wined, and learnt that the stage Director would be READING the part for the two performances that evening. The role of Vladimir in *Waiting for Godot* could hardly be described as a "cough and a spit", as he never, in fact, leaves the stage (except once to urinate, the dear old-fashioned thing), and bangs on fairly continuously for two hours. I could not imagine the customers at the two performances being best pleased, particularly as, Boxing Night being what it is, they'd all booked months previously.

It was a nightmarish evening, and the two audiences were stunned. The curious thing is that fewer people than usual crashed out, mainly, I imagine, because they could not believe their peepers. The poor Stage Director, dressed as a tramp, was careering over the stage at whim, reading from what seemed to us a not absolutely up to date script. A strong note of hysteria swept through the actors, and poor Peter Woodthorpe took a terrible beating. As this was his first professional job, he found it even more of a nerve-racking ordeal than we did. During the interval, it seemed unlikely that he would resume his stage career, having locked himself in his dressing-room and, despite everyone's efforts, refused to emerge. Eventually, I winkled him out by telling him that he would be suspended by Equity if he didn't re-appear. I am happy to say that at no period in the evening did I use the nauseating phrase, "The show must go on", because this was a typical occasion when the show "mustn't go on", and everyone should have been given their money back.

Donald Albery, who wisely kept away from the theatre during the crisis, had sent two bottles of champagne for the company to wish them a Happy Christmas. I whipped through them at lightning speed as nobody else fancied them, and, in consequence, didn't fare too badly. Timothy was still in great pain, and I am bound to say, I rather hoped in my secret heart that he would be too ill to play the following day, because then they would have had to close the building, unless the lady stage manager was sent on to READ Mr Bateson's role, which would have given rather a novel twist to the play, and anyhow, I suppose I would have had to call her "Sow" throughout.

The next night's performances were even more nerve-racking than the previous two owing, in my case, to there being an absence of champagne, but we got through somehow, with glazed faces and terror and hate in our hearts. Egged on by Timothy Bateson, I rang up Mr Donald Albery and said that we would prefer that this sort of thing didn't occur again. I have to point out that I was not in a fearfully strong position at the time, as I had blackmailed him into letting me play the Ugly Duchess in a TV production of *Alice in Wonderland*. He had refused several times, and my agent could get nowhere with him. I was determined not to give up without a struggle, as the number of times a man is asked to play the Ugly D. are strictly limited, and as innumerable kind friends pointed out, there would be no need to put on anything other than a straight make-up.

But it was scheduled to be televised on the Sunday following Christmas and Mr Albery thought that it would be too much of a strain after the ten performances of *Godot* in Christmas

"I Know the Face, but . . ."

Week, and how right he was. At a party a few weeks previously I launched into a tiny guerrilla warfare. I started on Mr Albery early in the evening.

"Am I playing the Ugly Duchess?" I asked naïvely.

"No, you aren't, actually," he replied, with the ghost of a smile.

I popped up at regular intervals throughout the evening, and finally cornered him after a record number of negative encounters.

"You did say I could play the Ugly Duchess in *Alice in Wonderland*, didn't you, Mr Albery?" He muttered his assent in a series of expletives, and I went happily back to the lobster canapés.

So that was that. I was to regret his decision by the time I actually got to the B.B.C. Television Studios in Lime Grove. However, I am anticipating, and I must get back to the Great Godot Crisis. An actor had taken away a script over the Christmas week-end, with a view to understudying, and announced on Wednesday that he was willing to have a bash at Vladimir on Wednesday night. He was called Richard Dare, and was nothing short of a miracle. He got through superbly and we were in the clear again. But by that time, William Squire had been signed to open in the part in three weeks' time, and Paul Daneman had been asked to resume his original role until Squire was ready. It so happened that Paul Daneman had a few weeks off in between a film and embarking on the John Clements season at the Saville Theatre.

So we now had just the three Vladimirs in the offing, which was an advance on minus one. But this was to bring fresh difficulties and embarrassment. So successful was Richard Dare in the part that Paul Daneman, after a few rehearsals, was told he wouldn't be required, and I think Mr Albery would have quite happily got out of his contract with Mr Squire if he could have managed it. But Richard Dare deservedly got his break for

Waiting For Godot

his bravery, because directly William Squire joined our cast he disappeared to the New Theatre, also under Mr Albery's management, to take over the lead from Nigel Patrick in *The Remarkable Mr Pennypacker*. This left us without an understudy again for quite a time, and plunged us into a helpless rage once more.

It meant a great deal of rehearsing, and the ensuing weeks after Christmas were an appalling strain. The Saturday before *Alice in Wonderland*, I was attacked by a severe bout of laryngitis, and could hardly get through the two performances. I made the unfortunate Stage Director alter his secret report, which read, "Mr Bull hardly able to speak", to "Mr Bull seemed to be suffering from a slight cold". I did not want Mr Albery to stop my Ugly Duchessing at the last moment, and it was likely to affect all our chances of outside work for the remainder of the run. Discretion to let actors in West-End runs do broadcasts, TV, or open the Hanging Gardens at Derry & Tom's, is entirely in the hands of the management, and a strict employer can lose one a lot of side money.

My performance as the Ugly D. was pretty macabre, and must have frightened the bejesus out of the kiddy-winks. An ugly croak came out, and that was about all. But I got through, and really rather enjoyed the production. Gradually my voice came back during the following week, and apart from a severe rash which I got from my rubber wig, *Waiting for Godot* did not have any other startling effect until, in March, the last weeks of the run were announced, when we were all pretty near the end of our tethers, particularly those actually attached to one in the production.

We rang down on March 24th, 1956, after last-minute attempts at a transfer had failed. We had run eight months, and "Done it" nearly three hundred times. I packed my rubber wig away for the last time (or so I thought), and heaved a gigantic sigh of relief. I thought of thanking Mr Donald Albery publicly, by taking a small column in *The Stage*, and announcing: "Mr Peter Bull thanks Mr Donald Albery for a lucrative but not frightfully enjoyable engagement", but decided wisely against it. In fairness to Mr A. he did pop my salary up by five pounds a week, quite unexpectedly, and off his own bat, which made me feel half a heel when I went whirling up on my weekly visits to the British Actors' Equity Association to report, as deputy, on general conditions.

No one seemed madly anxious to employ me, and instead of going away, I hung about London trying to get a move on with my second book. My first, *To Sea in a Sieve*, had come out on February 27th, and to my amazement was bringing in some splendid dividends. It was then that a new vista opened. Perhaps I'd be able, in a few years' time, to retire from the stage to a lovely cottage in Kent with roses and paper backs littering the place, and a lot of old photographs of scenes from *Waiting For Godot*. But it was not to be yet. Suddenly, a Mr Michael Wide rang me up to ask if I would consider going out on a tour of *Waiting For Godot*. I told him he must be out of his tiny mind, and he said, oh no, he hoped to make a lot of money. He added then that Timothy Bateson and Peter Woodthorpe had said they'd do it if I did. I was frankly flabbergasted by the whole project, but suddenly thinking that it might be the funniest tour ever organised, I said I would. I asked for a percentage (knowing that the "returns" would ensure one good laugh per evening and certainly per matinée) and an armed guard to and from the Stage Door at the Grand Theatre, Blackpool, a wise precaution as you will see.

It was to be an eight weeks' tour, and at the end of the sixth I could give notice to quit. Three of the dates were in the London suburbs, so topographically it could not be so ghastly. It would also enable me to save a bit against my holiday which I was determined to take that year. Robert Eddison (with whom I hadn't acted since the disastrous *Boy David*), was to

Waiting For Godot

play Vladimir and Richard Scott was to direct. Rehearsals were held in the Chelsea Community Centre (handy for me, living just down the road), and I fear nice Mr Scott, who had hoped to give the play an entirely new production, was a bit disappointed to find that the gallant survivors not only wouldn't but couldn't alter their performance. It was a case of "*sauve qui peut*", and I was only concerned for Robert who had the heavy end to carry. But he rose triumphantly to the occasion a d went confidently and quietly about his business.

We opened at the Coliseum Theatre, Harrow, on May 21st, 1956, a house of entertainment we practically closed down. A few weeks later it was reconstructed into apartment houses. It was not an auspicious opening date, as the theatre resembled a tunnel, and back-stage conditions were bleak. There was no doorkeeper, no call-boy and no audience to speak of or even speak back. But we were able to get back to our respective homes in the evening and there was a frequent train service. I don't think any of the Harrovians slipped out of their dorms to "get the message", and it was only during this week that we discovered to our huge delight that Michael Wide's principal backer was none other than Miss Winifred Atwell, the ebullient and talented coloured boogie-woogie pianist. So this made it all right somehow. Her husband, who was also her business manager, used to ring up every evening at Harrow to ascertain the figures, and it was fortunate that the phone was between Master Bateson's and my dressing-room, so there was a rush to give them to him. Actually the first twice (if you know what I mean) he could not believe them at all, and when on the Friday we'd nosedived into the fifties, he thought there must be an error and we meant £250 odd. It was lucky that his wife was playing to around the £1,000 mark EVERY performance at that time in the Palladium.

We played to £499 12s. 10½d., so the cast did not get very much extra that week, but the Monday following we opened

"I Know the Face, but . . ."

at the Arts Theatre, Cambridge, which was to be quite a different pair of tramps. You would have thought by the laughter, bookings and general behaviour that we had brought the great Laughing Success of the Century to their doors and we played to virtual capacity. The running time went up by fifteen minutes in order to give the audience a chance to get over their apoplectic fits, and dons showed us round their collections of precious glass and things. We were patronised by the local theatre groups, who kindly interrupted their activities for a second to tell us what THEY were doing NEXT season, and Peter Woodthorpe (ex-Footlights star) had a great personal triumph on the stage, in the Press, and all over the street, which plunged Timothy and me in an orgy of beastliness to him. He took it in fairly good part and we pressed on to Blackpool.

Miss Attwell and her husband, to say nothing of Mr Wide, had been perked up considerably after the Cambridge week, only to be plunged into gloom by our sensational visit to the Lancashire seaside resort. It was to provide us with some unforgettable memories, and what possessed the management to book us in must be shrouded for ever in mystery. But even this cardinal error was eclipsed by their invitation to the Blackpool Old Age Pensioners to view *Waiting For Godot* at 1s. a head on the Monday night. It was soon apparent that this gesture was not far short of insanity. The O.A.P.s were very angry indeed, after the first few minutes, at not only having to witness *Waiting For Godot*, but also having to pay twelve pennies for the privilege. They determined to have their say, which meant that during the second act we couldn't have ours, so there was a bit of an *impasse*. Bedlam reigned, what with the banging of seats, yells of derision and one or two pertinent remarks when the tramps suggested hanging themselves. We started off with 700 persons in the Grand Theatre, and finished up with under 100. We took one quick curtain and there were rumours of the police being called out for "our special safety"

Waiting For Godot

as it says on some fire curtains. The awful thing is that I rather enjoyed the evening, as I had not needed a clairvoyant to tell me that Blackpool was not going to be one long triumph.

We were to do every penny of £444 on the week and we had a fairly alarming mid-week matinée. The Blackpudlians eyed us more than curiously in the streets, and one felt one should ring a leper's bell on approaching Boots the Cash Chemists to change one's library book. Mark you, the local Press went to town about the whole affair (it was slightly out of season anyhow) and rallied to our support. We were front-page news for the entire week. "*Godot* went through without interruption" or "There were two curtain-calls last night at the Grand Theatre" were typical sub-headlines and there was even a "leader" saying Blackpool didn't DESERVE to be sent shows like us and the Carl Rosa Opera Company, if they were going to behave like this. The truth of the matter was that poor Blackpool didn't deserve *Waiting for Godot*. In a city almost entirely devoted to sex-shows, oysters, plastic macs and the pursuit of pleasure, it was an anachronism to present such a piece there.

By the end of the week we were all a bit nervy and I couldn't wait to get out of the town. Even "Sex-drugged girls tell all" had turned out to be two giggly nudes; I had had one bad shrimp and been sick on the pier, so I decided to go to London that week-end, whatever the cost. Now to leave Blackpool on a Saturday night is a tricky assignment, as the only chance is to catch the 10.39 out of Preston, a city which lies about 15 miles out of Blackpool. Well, as the curtain of *Waiting For Godot* in theory didn't come down till 10.15, it was going to be a close shave, to put it mildly. But Master Bateson, who was taking part in the expedition, and I were by now desperate men and we were not going to be defeated by such a little obstacle as Time. We went to the Messrs Eddison and Woodthorpe, our tramp confederates, and asked them if they would be so kind as to leave out ALL the pauses in the play at the second house

"I Know the Face, but..."

on Saturday. Those of you who saw the play will remember that the pauses occupied most of the play. But even the artistes were staggered by the results. We whipped through the play and cut just the twenty minutes out of the play that night, and it was, I think, My Most Enjoyable Evening In the Theatre. It was, oddly enough, the only performance that seemed to go remotely well in Blackpool and, needless to say, we were on the verge of maniacal laughter throughout. Pozzo and his slave made every entrance and exit as if they were Belita and Chattaway at the height of their powers, and after their disappearance in the first act one tramp had to comment in the course of the play:

"Well, that passed the time."

"It would have passed in any case," is the reply.

"Yes, but not quite so rapidly," says the first tramp, which on this occasion was said with such meaning that they both started to go off into paroxysms, only stopped by the Messrs Bateson and Bull making threatening gestures from the wings.

We had a car waiting for us and, with most of our make-up still on, tore through the night only to find that we had ten minutes to spare at Preston station.

After this, the Pavilion Theatre, Bournemouth, was the Department of Anti-Climax, and we sent most of the inhabitants off into a deep sleep. Very comfortable seats and the sea air took away all the unpleasantness and, as usual, I stayed at the Seamoor Commercial Hotel and Café (prop. J. Gourlay) which costs, or did, under four pounds all in for actors. The Gourlays are sweet and kind, and though there was a permanent TV show through the supper (until mercifully kibitzered by Mr Bateson's naughty feet getting entangled in the wires), it was also what is known as A Good Pull-Up for Carmen, which meant that one had a CHOICE in the evenings, which made a splendid change from ordinary digs where the plate is plonked in front of you william-nilliam. Also we had the use of their bathing-hut, which helped us through the week, during which we jolly nearly touched four figures.

Then gently down the coast to Brighton, where we were back to banging of seats and a certain amount of confusion. There was a night when a retired military gent could be heard inexplicably shouting above the turmoil: "No wonder we lose the colonies if they put on drivel like this", but we passed the £1,000 mark and the Headmaster of Lancing liked it (or so he said).

The next two weeks we were to play in the suburban theatres of London. It was delightful living at home again, and this comfort easily compensated for the appalling business we did at the gigantic Streatham Hill Theatre, where they threw pennies on the stage on the first night, but never into the box-office during the week. It was nice to move on to Golders Green the following week, where people seemed to enjoy the play for a change, and I had a dressing-room with a star on the door. This week we all started speaking to each other again, after losing our heads to such an extent in the purlieus of Streatham that notes were being left at the stage door.

Our lady patron, Miss Winifred Atwell, came to the matinée at Golders Green and seemed delighted with her property, though she carped a bit at the interval music. She thought it would be more in keeping with the mood of the piece to play some serious stuff (Schubert's "Valse Triste" was a suggestion), but I did point out that the audience at most suburban and provincial theatres, to say nothing of the orchestras concerned, would leave in a body if *The Desert Song* and *The Student Prince* didn't pop up in the repertoire at least once a month.

I gave in my notice at Golders Green, but said I would play the extra week at Birmingham which had been tacked on to the end of the tour by this time. We were all beginning to feel the strain by now, and even Robert Eddison said he could not go on for more than a week after we all left. We played at the

"I Know the Face, but..."

Birmingham Repertory Theatre, which is a charming bandbox of a theatre and I would love to be there in happier circs. There is also a table-tennis set in the wardrobe which makes it perfect. The resident company were away on a foreign tour and we were to fill the gap for two weeks. The booking was tremendous (the theatre only held about 600) and we were listened to in reverence and fairly stunned silence. In a way it was almost more maddening than hate and interruptions, but I was by now in a psychological state about the whole thing. We all found ourselves unable to speak to each other much off the stage, and the words came out automatically with even less meaning than they had had originally. I found the fortnight lying very heavily on my hands and could not wait for the final night of all.

Timothy and I caught the night train out of Birmingham, after having enjoyed one of the most expensive but happy dinners imaginable. It was July 28th, 1956, a year almost to the day since we had started at the Arts. We felt so relaxed and relieved that we could only smile stupidly at each other as we bundled out in the dawn of Euston Station. Yet although we were able to throw off the physical side of *Waiting For Godot*, in my case certainly it was to haunt my memory for many a long month, as indeed Mr Hobson had prophesied.

In a casual assessment I would say that being in it did me far more good than any other performance I have ever given, and only a few weeks ago I was asked to do a Shell-Mex advertising film for TV and use my *Godot* voice, whatever that meant. I was asked to speak on the play to the British Drama League, an invitation which I fear they regretted, owing to the subsequent gibberish that poured out of my mouth.

I hadn't been back a week before dear Mr Donald Albery, who must have watched our meanderings round with the keenest enjoyment, was on the blower asking my reactions to a six weeks' season at the Comedy Theatre to lure the American tourists. I said that I would want £1,000 a week and two

TRAINED nurses in attendance, and he didn't seem to think it was worth all THAT.

And although this is the end of that particular little section of my life, I have a lurking suspicion way back in my noddle that I shall end my days playing Pozzo in some of the less accessible repertory theatres of England. But heaven and the theatre-goers of Britain forbid!

Chapter XI

"I KNOW THE FACE, BUT..."

IT happens several times a week, and I don't mind telling you that I am sick of it. There I am, walking quietly along minding my own business and suddenly the way is blocked by one or more total strangers. A conversation ensues which generally begins with one of these gambits:

"Excuse me, but aren't you on the telly?"

or:

"I know you, don't I?"

or:

"I've seen YOU, but you haven't seen ME";

or (worst of all):

"Aren't you the B.B.C. Television artiste?" as if acting for the TV was the only possible medium for an actor.

I find now that, instead of pretending that they are talking gibberish, or that one is Lithuanian, it is quicker and less embarrassing just to say, "Yes". Then, with any luck, they say: "Thought I was right", triumphantly to their companion(s) and push off. But sometimes there is an awkward pause, and they stare and stare, and with a bashful smile say:

"Excuse me, but I've forgotten your name. I know the face but——"

"Peter Bull," one replies.

There is a moment's dazed silence.

"Oh," they say in a tone that leaves one mortified, and they go away as quickly as possible.

I suppose I would rather have even this, though, than to be mistaken for Orson Welles, Robert Morley, Elwyn Brook-Jones or Alexander Gauge, even if I do like Walls' Sausages. But the

"I Know the Face, but . . ."

whole point is that you can appear in a successful play or a notable film and no one would stop you in the street to discuss them. The TV viewer is quite differently constructed from the ordinary human being, and because he, she, or it has seen you in their private or public houses, they think that they have a perfect right to accost you in a public thoroughfare or vehicle, though a lot of people get arrested for this sort of thing every day.

They will issue communiqués about what They thought of the play or some other offering, and I have had complete strangers start off by saying, "That was a bloody awful thing you were in last night", a statement that cannot lead to a binding friendship. They will ask you what Gilbert Harding is Really Like, and if you can get them seats for "The Army Game". The only time that I have been sympathetic to the viewer was during the rationing period, when my very existence depended on the magic idiot-box. At the big grocery store where I deal (no names, no free packets of Daz) I had only to appear in a serial for eggs, butter and bacon to spring from under the counter; but an unwise decision to display my talent in a play about Pontius Pilate brought me to near-starvation That Week. And this was in spite of the fact that it was written by the author of *Worm's Eye View*.

And so I long with a bitter-sweet nostalgia for the old days before the war when it was called Television and not "the telly", and when a mere handful of people had sets. In fact, the only person whom I knew for certain to be looking in was the mater, who was closeted in the Gramophone Shop in Sloane Street, where they were indulgent enough to let her watch indefinitely her youngest son capering. The transmissions all took place from the Alexandra Palace, which is such a bizarre building anyhow that it all seemed like a dream and took a lot of one's nerves away particularly on Saturday, when one could use all the impedimenta which surrounded the Ally-Pally, like

"I Know the Face, but . . ."

boating ponds, miniature railways and "try your luck" booths.

I worked there happily quite a lot from 1936 to 1939, mainly with Dallas Bower, Jan Bussell and Fred O'Donovan, who were pioneers and have never received the credit they deserved. The difficulties of production in those days were immense, and I shall not easily forget a series of revues (Dallas Bower in charge) which starred Nelson Keys, Hermione Baddeley and sometimes Valerie Hobson, exquisitely calm and collected and singing her way free of the horror films in which she had lately been screaming her guts out in Hollywood. I was generally Mr Keys's stooge, an alarming assignment, as he couldn't or wouldn't learn the lines of the sketches, and I had to keep my head sufficiently to give him one or two feed lines and if possible bring the sketch to some sort of conclusion.

But since the war a deadly seriousness has crept into television, and with the competition between the rival channels it is difficult to approach any engagement light-heartedly. I find it far and away the most tiring and least rewarding of the media, and I have appeared in countless productions, some of which I would be wise to forget. Occasionally something pops up that has a grain of originality and excitement about it, and there is one gentleman for whom I would do a lot, called Michael Mills. He was, and is now again, one of the few people in the Corporation who believes in attempting the impossible and sometimes coming within an ace of achieving it.

One of his shows was a mammoth biography of Miss Marie Lloyd, in which he had the assistance of Miss Pat Kirkwood. The phrase "she's a trouper" now has an old-fashioned and faintly derogatory air and is usually bandied about when someone continues to play with a high temperature or a shattering bereavement. Miss Kirkwood has certainly played under hese conditions, but it is her unselfishness, lack of conceit, enormous guts, and above all a shining talent, that made her for me a "trouper de luxe". Although we had rehearsed for

"I Know the Face, but . . ."

weeks in a dreary drill-hall in Shepherds Bush, as usual everything seemed totally different in the studio when we came to the dress rehearsals. *The Story of Marie Lloyd* was to be the biggest musical ever staged on TV and the sets were found to be so numerous and elaborate that a lot of them had to be stored outside the studio and rushed in at the last moment. Miss K. had just the thirty changes of costume, and on the final run-through had no time to make several of them. I was playing her manager and frequently found myself having to make faces into the camera and hoping that she would arrive before I had exhausted my repertoire. Other tiny problems that Patricia had to face were that (*a*) the orchestra was housed in another studio and she had therefore to sing her innumerable songs to a distant "play-back"; (*b*) there was no space for a promised quick-change room, with the result that she found herself dressing and undressing between two rows of hanging wardrobes, which involved delightful voyeuring for the gents manipulating the lights on the gantry above; (*c*) after singing any songs in the theatre set she had to jump down off the back of the stage, as frequently there was no ladder there to assist her.

Now a great many stars would have screamed "murder" and insisted on some of the risks being eliminated, but not our Miss Kirkwood. After two chaotic dress rehearsals I seriously thought they might have to substitute *Victory at Sea* or some other filmed stand-by, but Miss K. seemed unflustered and so devoid of panic that a sort of dotty enthusiasm spread through us all, and quite suddenly we were back in a theatre proper before an exciting first-night. Although the show overran its time by forty minutes, and there were mishaps too numerous to mention, some of the results were remarkable, and it is interesting to note that the second transmission a few days later (shortened, tidied and slick) was nowhere near as effective.

Miss Kirkwood did all her changes, and it was with enormous

"I Know the Face, but . . ."

relief that I caught out of the corner of my eye Marie Lloyd slipping under the camera lens and coming to sit by me with no seconds to spare, and throughout the two hours one was overwhelmingly conscious of a superb artiste dashing around like a mad thing, but giving a performance of enormous attack and charm. There was a remarkable happening to end the evening which is especially memorable. In the closing moments of the play Marie Lloyd dies on stage after singing "I'm one of the ruins that Cromwell knocked about a bit". She has clutched the curtains to try and steady herself and falls to screams of laughter from the audience who think it is all part of the act. She is left lying on the stage, and the next scene on TV was the front of her little suburban house with the curtains being drawn by her housekeeper (Nora Nicholson) to denote her passing. A messenger boy rides up on a bicycle with some flowers:

"For Miss Marie Lloyd," he announces.

"But she's———" the housekeeper starts to say, but the boy has bicycled away whistling one of the late Miss Lloyd's songs, "Follow the Band". The scene fades and the whole cast take up the melody very quietly, rising to a crescendo at the end. Titles and credits flash on the screen, and the "all clear" signal is given in the studio. We look around, but there is no sign of Miss Kirkwood. Suddenly she appears breathless but beautiful from behind the makeshift changing-room, and the whole studio breaks into a frenzy of clapping and cheering. It was, I think, the most spontaneous tribute to a "trouper" that I can remember. Why she has never re-enacted the part in the proper theatre I shall never understand.

My next adventure with Michael Mills was in a series of scripts written by the late Ted Kavanagh, and starring another splendid artiste, viz. Bobby Howes. They were in the shape of a series of revues dealing with the trials and tribulations of "the little man". There was a resident chorus; and Mr Howes, a gorgeous lady called Eve Ashley, and I, were the resident com-

"I Know the Face, but . . ."

pany. The series was entitled "Such Is Life", and was, I gather, a bit too sophisticated for the ordinary viewer. But I did learn more in my brief sojourn as the Menace in Mr Howes's life than I have learnt in most of my stage career. It is an enormous help to be performing in a hazardous medium like television with an actor who is equal to any emergency and who can, when things go wildly wrong, say or do something that not only saves the situation but is also dead in character. I had never acted in this sort of thing before, and I viewed it all with apprehension, but Mr Howes was enchanting to me and really quite sorry that he had omitted to answer a fan letter I had written him in 1931 anent a performance of his in a show called *Sons of Guns*. He used to come to my flat in Wellington Square (commonly known as "Sordid Hall"), and I showed him that my fanship was genuine by the comprehensive collection I had of his records. The only one I didn't possess was "She's my lovely", which he gave me. There were several highly risible episodes in the series, and in one I played a dentist who held Mr Howes captive in a chair. I had a hilarious time whizzing him up and down on the foot treadmill, singing "Today I am So Happy" and other gay tunes, while he writhed in agony.

Towards the end of the series, Michael Mills was informed by the Corporation that he had overspent his allocation of money and as a result could not be given a chorus for the last episode. To compensate, after bribery and corruption, I was put into full drag, first as a seaside landlady and then in a gorgeous evening dress which had been previously worn by Miss Mai Bacon, whom curiously enough I strangled in a later television production. I played the part of Miss Eve Ashley's mother, and the gentleman dressers at Lime Grove were not unpleased by this transvestist carry-on and loaded me down with so many jewels that I could hardly move. I was finishing off a film with George Raft at the time, and the day after the transmission, gave him Miss Ashley's love.

"I Know the Face, but..."

"Oh," said Mr Raft. "Where did you see her?"

"I was playing her mother last night on TV," I replied smoothly, which held Mr Raft for the whole morning, and I kept on seeing him giving me even more menacing looks than usual.

I suppose the most frightening experience I have had in television was in a short thriller entitled *Change Of Air*, in which I starred on Whit Monday 1957. It was written by Berkeley Mather, who is really a retired high-ranking Army gent. who specialises in Soho low-life stories. I read the script, in which the principal character was called Maximilian Bull, a coincidence, allied with the charm and persuasion of Mr Mather, that forced me to take the proposition seriously. It was a half-hour Grand Guignal about a paranoiac "fence", who kept a large country house for hiding diamonds, mink and other loot in. The part of Mr Bull was written in Soho-ese, and was meant to be dead common. One of my disadvantages as an actor has been my total inability to speak any dialect other than rather affected ordinary English. The moment I attempt an accent of any sort I run into trouble, and a mass wince is registered by my director and fellow artistes. If you've never seen a mass wince you've missed a frightening sight. Usually I'm allowed to lapse back into my normal voice, if they can't find a replacement in time.

So I viewed *Change Of Air* with horror, and told Mr Peter Lambert, the director, that I could only do it "straight". The maddening thing was that the author said I could play it any way I liked and could alter the script according to taste. I could think of no other way of withdrawing from the engagement until I suddenly had a brainwave. Although I had to do all the talking in the piece, the part of my henchman was desperately important, as I had to talk the pants off him, throttle him and finally push him down a trap-door.

"I'll only do it," I said airily to Peter Lambert, "if Sammy

"I Know the Face, but . . ."

Kydd plays Frisky" (the henchman). Sammy and I had worked on the TV serial of *Pickwick Papers* as Mr and Master Weller, and as he's about the nicest person in the world, apart from being splendid to work with, he is never out of a job. So I thought I was quite safe. To my horror he was free for the week in question.

"If you think I'm going to miss this," Sammy said on the blower later, "you're very much mistaken."

We had four and a half days in which to rehearse, and it frankly wasn't enough. To my dismay, I was allowed to run riot, contrary to usual procedure. Normally, TV directors follow you about like detectives, making extraordinary faces and looking through their legs to see that you aren't an inch out from the camera point of view.

But I wasn't even allowed the possible alibi of constriction.

"Don't worry about the cameras," said Lambert. "They'll follow you."

At the end of the second day I was pretty certain that I could not learn the lines in time (it was practically a monologue of thirty minutes' duration). Sammy took me home, where we horrified his wife (Pinky), with whom I have a good deal in common as she is an ex-table tennis champion. We went through it countless times, but I did get into a ghastly tizz and had to borrow some tranquillizers from a doctor-actor friend of mine. I made myself a burden to my nearest and dearest, who had to hear my lines at all times of the day and night, and shuddered as I reached the more extravagantly purple patches.

"Why are you worrying?" they said, some of them. "It's Bank Holiday and only seven million will be looking in."

I hurriedly bought my *TV Times*, which divulges the rival firms' wares. This slightly raised my morale, as while I would be doing my "nut" and my probable swansong for Auntie BBC, the ITV would be showing H. Bogart in *The Maltese Falcon*. Surely there could be no choice. Which would you watch,

"I Know the Face, but..."

chum? It was a brief respite, but all the week-end I was jangling with nerves and trying to live on other people's. Came the dawn of Whit Monday, and I took a No. 11 bus to Shepherds Bush and felt as cool and as calm as a very fat cucumber. For some unknown reason I was quite happy and absolutely certain that I was not going to appear in *Change Of Air* that evening. I was helped in this fantasy by the fact that the trap-door, through, into and under which the whole of the action took place, would neither open nor shut during all the run-throughs. Mine was a very strenuous part, and at one period I had to start throwing Mr Kydd down into the cellar and dash over to the far end of the studio, where Mr K's double had already begun to roll down the steps, and I had to follow him. As the second set represented the steps down the cellar itself, I had to climb up a tiny ladder to get to the top. This needless to say, broke during the second run-through, which didn't help my confidence. About this time, I felt my voice going, so I told the director that another complete run-through was unwise. Owing, however, to the eccentric behaviour of the trap-door, it was thought advisable to have a final crack. I was to save my voice, he said, and off we went until I found myself croaking the last few lines.

"I've lost my voice," I cheerfully croaked to the control-room.

"Goodness," said Peter Lambert, "so you have."

There was no time to say "told you so" to him, and we paid a visit to the resident nurse, who naturally was quite unperturbed. She wasn't going to play Maxie Bull for seven million viewers in two hours. She advised gargling, which I did a bit of, and turned my croak into a choke. So with a choky croak I left the building for the local hospital in order to search for a miracle cure. P. Lambert kindly escorted me in a taximeter-cabriolet, and said he would take it out of expenses. I thought this Fair. We arrived at the hospital, where a rather giggly,

"I Know the Face, but . . ."

pretty nurse asked me my age. I croaked that it didn't matter frightfully and could I see a doctor? There were a lot of people in the waiting-room, including a gent. who said he was looking forward to seeing me on his screen in a few hours. I whispered that he might very possibly see me, but it was unlikely that he would hear me.

A doctor came in, looking rather like Dirk Bogarde, and after a few seconds opined that I had lost my voice. I agreed with him, and what was he going to do about it? He asked me if I'd gargled, and I said I had gargled. I whispered that my career rather depended on his ministrations and had he not something magical which would clear up my larynx for the next two hours and a half? After that, I did not care what happened, as I had only one future commitment. As this was a TV film in which the character was described as a "hoarse, Soho type", it just fitted in, as somebody almost certainly said to somebody. The doctor studied me for a few seconds, and said he had something in mind, but that it might paralyse my face. I whispered that perhaps it might be a bit dangerous, and alter my interpretation of the role. However, he vanished and came back in a couple of minutes with his face contorted (or was it my imagination?).

"I don't think *that's* a very good idea," he announced.

So he gave me a very strong gargle which made precious little diff., and a bottle of same and P. Lambert and I left the building. We had made the taxi wait, which was A Good Idea. Mr Lambert left me in gloom—I mean, he was in gloom. I was as merry as a grig, knowing that something quite extraordinary must happen. I went in to Sammy, who asked if there was anything he could do. I whispered that I would like to go for a long motor drive. So off we tootled. Half an hour later, we found ourselves back in my flat in Chelsea, zonking down the drink and, I regret to say, giggling at the thought of those waiting millions. I then went systematically through my medicine

"I Know the Face, but . . ."

cupboard, and finally found the vintage lozenges which I had brought back from America in 1951. They had congealed into an unhealthy mess, which looked like the remains of some person in a horror film, but I swallowed the lot. Sammy and I got back to Lime Grove very shortly before the transmission. He had given me a curious sense of security and I didn't exactly repay his devotion by knocking him sideway during the play. But until we were on the air, I did not speak at all again. As the last seconds passed I looked at the studio wall, where it said in illuminated letters: "Vision On—Sound On", and thought the latter supposition unlikely.

I went through the play without giving a damn. It is the only time that this has ever happened to me, and I suppose the best way to overcome nerves is by having a genuine physical complaint. Anyhow, kind friends point out that the whole thing is psychosomatic, whatever that may mean, and of course it is. It was certainly the most bizarre performance I have given in all my puff, and the immediate reaction surprised even me. In my opinion I had gone eighty-five times too far in my impersonation, even before laryngitis had set in, but the next morning I got flattering notices, Mr Henry Sherek offered me a job, and a great many intimate friends rang me up to compliment me on "The new voice I had put on", which all goes to show something or other. I had, for once, a trickle of fan mail, from what, I hope, cannot be described as the ordinary viewer. The fact that I had played a character called Bull seems to have convinced some of the correspondents that it was an autobiographical sketch out of my own life. I quote from one or two letters:

"Have you really got a trap-door in your house?"

"Have you been in prison?"

"Please get a signed photo of the two policemen."

"Why did you hit Mr Sam Kydd so hard?"

One of them finished impertinently:

"I Know the Face, but . . ."

"Answer soon, or I shall lose interest."

As the play had ended with me locked in my own cellar facing starvation and certain death, my acting cannot have been all that convincing, though I do think I would have qualified for the Kenneth Kent Scholarship for Attack, which R.A.D.A. dishes out annually.

One of the shortcomings of the viewers is the inconsistency of their hearing and seeing powers. One can go through a part with laryngitis and no one notices a thing, but stumble over a few words and the whole world has noticed. Recently I got in rather a muddle during a Children's Hour programme on a Sunday. I wasn't prompted, but went on talking gibberish until I remembered roughly the gist of what the author had given me to say. I hadn't been back home ten minutes before my supposed friends were on the blower. The kinder ones condoled, and the others gave me a far too vivid verbatim report of my flounderings. I suspect that some of them had tape-recorders concealed about their persons, and I coldly asked them what the hell they thought they were doing listening to the kiddywinks' hour on a nice Sunday afternoon. The knockout blow was administered by the commissionaire, who stands outside my club. He usually greets me with warm deference, but a few days after my débâcle, he was standing what my friend Mr Granger calls "po-faced" outside the swing doors. I had just emerged from the Turkish Baths and was feeling rather shaky. "Mr Peter," he said grimly, "I've got a bone to pick with you. You nearly fluffed your lines on Sunday."

This, apart from being the understatement of 1958, made me think of tendering my resignation from the club before I was blackballed, to coin a phrase. For how could I face Mr Ivor Brown in the swimming-pool after that?

Yes, it is the aftermath of a TV appearance which is so embarrassing. Years ago I was tickled pink when someone recognised me in the street. Now I go scarlet or ash-white, according

"I Know the Face, but . . ."

to the tone of the inquisitor. How would you like to be walking past Harrods and have people shout from the back of lorries?

"Hullo, strangler."

"Done anyone in today?"

I saw a policeman's eyebrows disappear right under his helmet, for how was he to know that I had been placing my hands around Catherine Boyle's pretty neck the night before in *Ladies in Ermine*? One is not even safe from children. After I had played Big Chief Sitting Bull, I had to hide in my basement and not venture out until dusk, or I would be pursued by tots twirling tommyhawks and yelling that they were out for my scalp.

I myself have only recently owned a television set. I always swore I would never have one, but a dear friend left it inside my front door the other day (he had purchased a brand new one), so there it sits in a corner of the room in which I am typing this nonsense, and it means that at 2.30 p.m. I will have to down tools, and "Watch With Mother". It makes work impossible, as I have to "Listen With Mother" at 1.45 p.m., which makes me feel like a bigamist. I am mad about the latter programme, because Daphne Oxenford usually asks if I am sitting comfortably. No one else ever asks me this, and I am deeply grateful. Fortunately, it's a v. old set, so I only get the BBC which makes friction with my Inner Self less strenuous. I cannot decide whether I class TV over or under cocaine as a drug, but goodness! how I resent the way it has affected some of my friends. You know the sort of thing! You are asked to drinks, and you hope for quiet stimulating conversation, and all you get is the unlicensed debauchery of "The 6.5 Special", and many's the dinner which has been ruined owing to the hostess's double preoccupation.

I find a tendency, when I am acting in TV, to let pictures swim up before my eyes of my chums watching ME. As I know

"I Know the Face, but . . ."

that a lot of them deliberately turn the sound off and/or distort "The Picture", so that one looks like a monster in science fiction, it doesn't make for confidence. So I try and keep my appearances secret from people like Robert Morley who, with his whole family, seems to be permanently glued to the machine. I remember on one occasion I was about to appear in something of which I was particularly ashamed, and thought I was going to get away with it, when early that Sunday morning the blower went and it was Mr Morley in person:

"We shall, of course, all be watching this evening."

"What do you mean by 'all'?" I asked, terrified.

"Only Carol Reed and the immediate family."

Now you can understand and why I have not as yet been in a C. Reed film. Sometimes Mr M. leaves it until after a production. The morning following my first appearance as Sam Weller's dad in *Pickwick Papers*, the phone went and a sepulchral voice said:

"Not everybody's idea of Tony Weller, dear," and rang off.

But he can be lavish in his praise, and sometimes it is comforting to think of him watching the screen and doing eight other things at the same time.

Amidst all this welter of abuse against the medium, I do remember with pleasure one or two productions which not only actually gave pleasure to people one respects, but which on reflection I almost enjoyed myself. There was, for instance, a version of *The Man Who Was Thursday* by G. K. Chesterton, in which I played the title role. It was directed by Jan Bussel, who now devotes all his time to puppets. On this occasion I was padded out to three times my already not inconsiderable size, and lowered from the studio roof in a balloon. Not a simple operation, which tested even the resources of the Kirby flying men, who usually have nothing heavier than the current P. Pan to cope with. P. Bull was a severe strain.

Then there was a highly advanced production by George

"I Know the Face, but . . ."

More O'Ferrall of *The Lady's Not For Burning*, which caused a blockage on the telephone at the Alexandra Palace Exchange by indignant viewers ringing up to ask why the BBC put on "such rubbish". It's a curious fact that the ratio is about ten thousand to one of people who ring up complaining to those who want to praise.

One of my big chances came (after Mr Robert Morley had turned it down) when I was asked to play George the Fourth in a play by Robert Kemp, called *The Honours of Scotland*. This dealt with a supposed visit to Edinburgh by England's wildly unpopular king. He apparently made the error of appearing at a reception in full highland regalia, and if you've ever tried to change from fairly ordinary clothes into THAT in two minutes flat, you will know what I was up against. My big scenes came when the king tore up his carefully prepared speech and spoke in his own halting words (money for old rope) what he felt about the whole thing. At the end of the speech the piper struck up the full bagpipe carry-on, and it wasn't a great help when the be-kilted gent (borrowed from a Highland regiment, and unable to attend any rehearsals owing to state duties) started to pipe up BEFORE the speech. My under-the-breath comment was v. unregal.

But these were only oases in a morass of bad plays, and hair-raising run-throughs and, as actors know only too well, it needs an iron constitution to face several weeks in a draughty, ill-heated drill hall in mid-December or Boys' Clubs half-way to Scotland with the Christmas decorations still up at the beginning of June. It takes several days for the strongest participant to recover from a major production, but of course it is useless to conceal from oneself that to survive as an actor one will have to work constantly in this medium. The theatre is more chancy than ever, with shows either running three years or three weeks (had two of the latter type in 1957), and the cinema is in a constant state of flux, but with luck someone will in-

"I Know the Face, but . . ."

vent a super TV pill which will make us sail through all our commitments with *panache*, confidence and even pleasure. Until this happens, we and the viewers will have to endure all hazards of the enterprise.

The other month I was travelling in a train to some ghastly touring date, and a man stopped me in a corridor. I was pretty startled when he said:

"Excuse me. Are you a freak?"

"Yes, I suppose I am, in a way," I replied meekly.

"No," he said; "I meant, are you Afrique, the impersonator?"

I replied in the negative.

"Thought you were," he said triumphantly, and trotted off quite happily, which all goes to show what an actor is up against.

CHAPTER XII

THE SUMMING-UP

AND that's it. I have no more to communicate, and I don't mind telling you that I have been dreading this chapter. You see, as I read and re-read the extraordinary hotch-potch which I have written, I become increasingly conscious of what you, the reader, are thinking. I have been trying to use you as a judgement-seat, and I can see where I have gone desperately wrong. I imagine you are asking yourself what the hell all the fuss is about. There is for you no question of what I should do. It has become obvious that I have no right to remain on the stage if I treat it all with such levity. I have without doubt proved that I am not ambitious, efficient or able to make any outstanding contributions to the arts.

So why don't I just shut up about it, and either take shares in a launderette or a coffee-bar, and go on writing spasmodically? You are absolutely justified in your exasperation, and in a few minutes I AM going to shut up, but there are one or two conclusions that I have reached which are deeply disturbing to ME.

The first is that, despite the apparent way I have treated my life on the stage, I still feel that I have not wasted my time, even if I have wasted yours. This comforting thought is entirely due to the conviction that in no other profession would I have had the opportunity of meeting such generous, fascinating, amusing, maddening and delightful people. I am gregarious by nature and love my fellow-creatures. I could not be less self-contained, with the result that I regard friendships and the satisfaction they bring as almost the most important thing in life. The pleasure that I have derived from them has, I am sure,

The Summing-up

robbed me of any bitterness or remorse that so often attacks those who have not quite made the grade. Also the satisfaction of attaining my few ambitions so early on helped me to relax, and not take desperate measures to achieve something which was probably out of my grasp anyhow.

My only twinge of real conscience comes to the surface when I think of how much farther I could have got if I had learned my job properly in the first place. At no period during my career have I worked at curing the more serious faults which I possess as an actor and I have never even taken the trouble to seek outside help. If I had done all this, there is no doubt that I would have gained the confidence to display my wares in public with more keenness. But, to be truthful, I never at any time had any illusions about becoming a star or even a first-class actor.

The fact remains, however, that economically I have managed not only to remain on the stage for a quarter of a century, but also to enjoy earning my living at this particular job. I am not referring to the actual business of "acting", but to "being in the theatre", two very different facets of the profession. To go into the vulgarity of figures, I have never earned more than £2,000 a year (always excepting the Hollywood excursion in 1938) and I have usually stuck around the £1,500-or-less mark. I have twice lost my all in managerial ventures and would do the same to-morrow if an opportunity occurred, and I cannot pretend that there is any security in the future. Indeed, as I write this there is not a sniff of anything on the horizon, and it is quite clear that if I had any responsibilities, marital or filial, I would have no hesitation in cutting my losses and leaving the business.

Which brings one back to the problem that I faced you with at the beginning of this book. I am already half in "another business", and without this vague promise of additional income, I would be facing the future with something like despair. As

"I Know the Face, but . . ."

it is, I am in danger of falling between at least two stools. I can either continue applying myself to both careers or abandon the stage, and all that it means, for writing. There is at the moment no half-way house, though I remember thinking, when my first book was published, how I would be able to turn down the jobs that had no immediate appeal. Owing to the rise in the cost of living, foolscap and public transport, it doesn't seem to have worked out like that at all. In fact, I cannot remember when I last turned down an offer, if out of employment at the time.

As to the enjoyment of acting, perhaps at the back of my mind I have a fantasy that I will one day actually catch myself looking forward to "doing" it, but I still appear to myself to have no normal feelings about the stage at all. I have never caught myself thinking or saying, "I'd give my right arm to play So-and-So", and I am totally unable to identify myself with the sort of actor who does. My stage life seems so totally alien from my ordinary one that if I go to a matinée of some play in which I am naturally not appearing that evening, I find it impossible to believe that it is I who will be up on another stage later on, in front of probable paying customers. The mere thought unnerves me and I find it difficult to be in the audience without worrying.

It cannot be a healthy thing for an actor to confess that even the prospect of a whacking great new part in a new play does not thrill him to the marrow, and it is humiliating to confess that I would rather have a small, though showy (I will admit), role for which the only attribute required is my peculiar personality. As to the strain and tension attached to a new job, I find this does not lessen with the years. Long before the first night I retire behind a curtain of misery and yearn for it all to be over, and I can creep back into my bed after the ordeal. I am not denying that every actor feels a bit of this and there is usually something radically wrong with one who doesn't. I am only saying that it affects me abnormally, and when I say a

The Summing-up

prayer before an opening, it is never: "Please let me be good and have smashing notices", but; "Please let me get through" (*period*). This attitude is defeatist to a degree and shows lack of guts, ambition and confidence, all of which qualities should be compulsory in an actor. The silly thing is that I have never (up till now) had total personal disaster on the stage, and if catastrophe strikes from another quarter I become positively heroic. It is I who help people who have "dried", improvise speeches, hold up scenery, go and fetch props forgotten, and in fact suddenly I turn into a "regular little trouper". But even with this reassuring evidence I would still have been happier not to have been on that particular stage at all in those circumstances.

I suppose my ideal medium would have been the silent films. I could then have made all "my faces" and not gone into a frenzy about "lines". It's not that I'm lazy about the latter, as I usually go to the other extreme and for weeks carry about on my person filthy bits of paper on which I've written my part, to study at odd moments. If I am in a play I go over my part before every perf., though after a few weeks that surely shouldn't be necessary. The result is that quite often I get to the stage on the stage where I am thinking of my next line but one, which spells disaster for the actor and disconcerts his fellow-artistes.

Also this is probably visible to the more perceptive members of the audience who know instinctively that it's an actor's technique to "lose himself" in a part, and how can he do this if he is constantly thinking if it's his turn to speak and what to say? The chances of him appearing natural are remote. I now know to my cost when I am relaxed and in fact being any good at all. The two performances in recent years, which I do not view with shame in retrospect, were in *Figure of Fun* and *Waiting For Godot*: at first sight, perhaps, two wildly dissimilar roles, but to me they were both like jumping into a deepish

"I Know the Face, but . . ."

swimming-pool and having to swim for dear life. There was just no time to think what the next line was, let alone the line after next. Both of the performances were "trick", in that once I had stumbled on A Way To Play them, the director could not or would not stop me, as he realised the only chance of my getting through would be on a wave of self-confidence. Curiously they were accounted "difficult" assignments, and I had the added advantage of not being able to visualise what some other actor would have made of them.

Therein is the clue to my lack of confidence. I can usually never believe that they haven't attempted to get every large character actor in London before trying me. Consequently, all through rehearsals I am certain to imagine that the director, the management and, worst of all, my fellow-actors are whispering behind their fans:

"Oh, if only they HAD got So-and-So playing it."

With the two roles mentioned it was slightly different, as they were so bizarre that they fell into no category. In them I could lose all restraint and do the opposite of "natural acting". They proved to me that wildly eccentric characters are my *forte* and I should stick to them when possible. With the opportunity for "unnatural" acting I can stop embarrassing myself and all concerned, and therefore should only play sex-maniacs, dope fiends, ordinary "maddies" or Ugly Duchesses. With these I automatically shed all inhibitions and can even be effective in a macabre way. But this is only if the director keeps me on a very loose rein. If he frowns and tries to curb me, I slip immediately back into a morass of insecurity. The consequence of this is that I am naturally hell for the imaginative director, who has planned lovely and intricate things for me to do, which I am usually totally incapable of carrying-out, owing to my "Method" of self-expression. My seeming lack of co-operation is not pig-headedness or the result of conceit and/or crass stupidity, as the director would be justified in surmising. It's

The Summing-up

just inadaptability, as no one, let's face it, actually enjoys bursting into tears in front of a company one likes and admires or indeed, come to think of it, a company one hates and despises. But dear Sir John Gielgud made me do this very thing during the rehearsals of *The Lady*, and though I would have given a great deal to be able to do it as he wanted, I found it beyond my powers.

Against all these limitations I am undeniably lucky in the possession of a curious, and to put it as kindly as possible, an off-beat face. No other actor resembles me, so when a part comes up for casting which fits no pre-conceived idea of what is required, some indulgent director thinks it might be amusing to have me. As often as not, I am then asked to "read" the part before any decision is reached. I endeavour to side-step this, as I always think it's an unfair and injudicious method of casting. I know several very fine actors who can hardly string two words together at first sight. Like them, I attempt to settle for a week's trial at rehearsal and say that if I prove wanting, I'll pop off with no umbrage and no money. Both the director and I can usually tell after a few days if there is any likelihood of a satisfactory engagement.

This attitude of mine only applies to the stage proper. In the cinema and certainly the television world I am perfectly willing to have a bash at the most wildly unsuitable parts, if I happen to need the money at the time. And this brings me to another divergence of outlook from other members of my profession. I cannot see the point of starving for a principle. If I need the cash *instanter*, I am incapable of turning down a job because the salary and billing, to say nothing of the part, are not quite what one had hoped for; and phrases like "Offering an actor in my position that sort of money" or "wouldn't give me the billing, old boy" seem gibberish to me, if the bailiffs are at that moment hammering on the door. Half the bitterness, chips on shoulders and elsewhere, and dropped or drooping

"I Know the Face, but..."

corners of mouths, seem to be the fruits of this lunatic philosophy.

Certainly a lot of people could turn round to me and say: "Look where your attitude's got you." And they would be dead right in their conclusions, particularly when I think of my performance as a Siberian Gold Merchant (pretend) in *Dixon of Dock Green* recently. But against this seeming folly I would like to point out that I am not in debt, am reasonably contented, and am not going round saying that I ought to be playing the Rex Harrison part in *My Fair Lady*.

I also hasten to add that I am not including the star or feature player in my analysis, as they have to be very careful over decisions. An unwise one can do irreparable damage. I am really thinking mainly of those who have missed the big boat and won't even try to get into the dinghy. They sit at home or in their clubs waiting for the sensational offer to come, and not daring to accept a lesser one in case it might clash.

I love the majority of my fellow-actors immoderately, but I am the first to admit that they can be infuriating, puerile and, on occasions, as intelligent as moths. It is when they start discussing their careers and their agents that claustrophobia and irritation set in with me. The theme "My Agent" is a conversational Must, whenever two actors on amicable but not intimate terms meet.

"My Agent is the most iniquitous, most wonderful, wickedest, sharpest, slowest, laziest, crookedest, silliest, cleverest, best, worst in London": I have never heard anyone talking about their agents except in superlatives, and I don't think I remember any actor just saying that they had a satisfactory agent.

"I can't imagine why I employ an agent," is a phrase used pretty non-stop.

I know exactly why I employ one, and I don't envy any of the twenty-odd ladies and gents who have tried to sell me to prospective employers in the last twenty-five years. I certainly

The Summing-up

don't grudge them the 10 per cent which they get for handling what might be larkily called "my business". I would rather (only don't tell them) give them 20 per cent than discuss terms myself. As to fixing "the billing", the mere idea of it gives me the shudders and in most cases I prefer to remain anonymous; unlike the star who was caught outside a West-End theatre, measuring the posters with a foot-rule, to see if his name took up more space than that of his co-star.

Another conversational waste of time with actors is discussing what photograph they are to insert in *Spotlight* (the actor's catalogue of wares for casting purposes). Your friend brings round a pile of pictures, showing him or herself in various clothes, make-ups, poses and hair-do's. You wade religiously through them and eventually choose one which you like.

"Do you think so? Funny," is your friend's only comment. You choose another.

"Um," says your friend. "Charles liked that one. I think it's awful." At the end of two hours they disappear, oozing gratitude and saying you have saved their life; and a totally different photograph from any you have liked appears in the next issue of *Spotlight*.

Another curious trait that most actors (including myself) possess is a total inability to understand why friends sometimes don't come round backstage after a performance. This invariably leads to unpleasantness of some sort.

"He, she or they can't have liked me, us or it."

"Extraordinary behaviour not coming round."

"Peter, Sybil, John or Jeannette have changed since they got into that TV quiz game," and so on.

What we never seem to realise is that their non-appearance after the show was due to the fact that either (*a*) they were with someone who had an epileptic fit and had to be taken home during the show, or (*b*) they had only limited time to catch their train to Guildford, or (*c*) they had loathed every

"I Know the Face, but . . ."

second of it and hesitated to come round and say so, or (d) they had been so moved that they were going straight home to write a fan letter, or (e) they had just finished an affair with another member of the company and didn't want to run the risk of running into him or her backstage, or (f) they didn't know we knew they were in front and hated going round anyhow.

I personally dislike going backstage intensely. I find I am absolutely tongue-tied and unable to express my pleasure if I *have* loved it and incapable of saying, "It's wonderful", if I've had an unenjoyable evening. I can now, with age, no longer even bring myself to say, "It's been a most interesting evening", which used to be my stand-by conversational gambit on these occasions. For these reasons I try to avoid going to first nights and taking part in the attendant tralala. I even dislike running into friends on ordinary nights and having to dissect or analyse what one is seeing. It always seems to end in subterfuge and betraying oneself.

But against all these idiosyncrasies of actors there are a thousand virtues, and I would like to try and point out to the layman the merits of those connected with this irresistible but heartbreaking profession. The difficulty is how to make you see actors as human beings. The headlines, scandals, confessions, marriages of those in the entertainment industry, which form such a feature of our daily press, have nothing to do with the creative endeavour and courage needed to produce a notable performance or production. The acute pleasure given by a performance of genius like Olivier's *Entertainer* or Guinness's in *The River Kwai* are totally unrelated to what became of Miss Diana Dors' strong-box in the Brompton Road. Yet a section of the public cannot rationalise the entertainment world, and because we are primarily there for their "entertainment", they try to fashion us according to their whim. They cannot or do not want to believe that hard work, discipline, and above all, immense talent are essential to the artist if he

The Summing-up

is to have a lasting effect on the industry or indeed posterity.

They would rather have it that an actor's life is a bed of roses, grossly overpaid, oversexed and possibly overdrugged. They quite fail to realise that the stars who stay the course have disciplined themselves probably more completely than leaders of other professions. The path to lasting fame and success is so tricky and treacherous that many potential stars fall by the wayside, resorting to drink or at worst suicide if they cannot provide the stamina required. Time and again some talent burns itself out through too much devotion to work, and the actor with a touch of greatness must perforce face terrible loneliness and doubts as a result of the gift he knows he possesses. Nothing short of perfection will satisfy him, and he in consequence can rarely be satisfied.

When he reaches a certain pinnacle, he knows that he is being watched by millions and that public fancy can be fickle beyond belief. Not everyone wishes him well, and by becoming an international figure his privacy is invaded and it is bound to affect his private life. Fresh problems spring up, and he suddenly finds his entire existence threatened. The Press sometimes help, but more often hurt, because they know the sort of things the readers want to devour. A dull star is no good to them, so any tiny foible is seized on and blown up to an immense size. Now that columnists have reached a new high in impertinent survey, it is usually safe to conclude that a bitchy or cruel interview is the result of the star's diffidence or resentment at having to put up with infringement of privacy.

It is no time before myths and legends are being spread high and wide. So-and-so is "cold", "has a big head", or is "difficult". Often I have been about to work with a performer who has a reputation of being "difficult", only to find that the reverse was the case. Almost invariably the "difficult" actor or actress is highly expert, intolerant of inefficiency and stimulating to work with. It is the jumped-up "starlet" or disappointed near-

"I Know the Face, but..."

star, who is usually temperamental, rude, boring and lazy.

I have been honoured in friendship by some very distinguished members of the profession, and it is alarming to realise how my idea of them varies from the characters given them by the Press, or indeed some of their fellow-actors. Yet when I try to explain to others the qualities which I find so endearing and valuable, I tend to make them sound charming but ordinary and totally different from what the listener wants to hear. It is, I fancy, because so much of their make-up (I use the word in its unnatural sense) is normal that they are able to contribute so much to the art of acting. It is only those who exist solely for display to the public and self-exhibition, who cannot adjust themselves to living like human beings. This minority do not realise the full extent of the damage until late in their lives, when they find themselves facing emptiness and loneliness.

All this sounds pompous, I suppose, and you may feel that I am the last person in the world who should make these *pronunciamentos*, being probably the least dedicated actor in the business. But I do know that the main reason why I have stayed so long and happily in the theatre has been because I have been lucky enough to be on the receiving end of the warmth, humanity, generosity and gaiety that actors seem to generate. They are not creatures from another world, but they do have the power to purvey the magic that still makes the theatre world a fabulous one in which to live. It is the sense of pride and the joy of living which I have personally felt, when appearing with such purveyors of magic as Gielgud or Guinness, that has been so memorable and lasting.

Such is the power of this magic that I would rather go pottering ineffectually along in the hope that every decade I may land up in another *Lady's Not For Burning*, or playing a cough and a spit in another *Horse's Mouth*. I would rather be doing this than suddenly become a great industrial tycoon with power and millions. You might say reasonably that if I was a great I.T.,

The Summing-up

I could then fulfil my functions as a manager, and present great actors in great plays in great theatres; but it would not be the same thing, though better for everyone else. The ultimate satisfaction for an actor is to be on a stage or screen close to "the magic" and catch its glow and bask in its reflection. Only then can you hope to understand what any of it means, and you need to be granted one peep at this secret world and feel part of it, to be suddenly imbued with faith, a sense of security and above all to be in love with life again.

THE END

Because I've realised why I can't leave the stage.

INDEX

Me . . . *Pages* 1–219

www.ingramcontent.com/pod-product-compliance
Lightning Source LLC
Chambersburg PA
CBHW071610080526
44588CB00010B/1083